Late Bloomers

BRENDAN GILL

Late Bloomers

ARTISAN · NEW YORK

CONCEPT AND DESIGN BY DENNIS AND SUSAN FEIGENBAUM

Production director: Hope Koturo

PUBLISHED IN 1996 BY ARTISAN,
a division of Workman Publishing Company, Inc.
708 Broadway, New York, NY 10003

Library of Congress Cataloging-in-Publication Data
Gill, Brendan, 1914-
Late bloomers/Brendan Gill
p. cm.
ISBN 1-57965-108-9
1. Celebrities – Biography. 2. Aged – Biography.
3. Middle aged persons – Biography. 4. Success. I. Title
CT105.G47 1996
920′ 009′04 – dc20
[B]
Printed in Hong Kong
10 9 8 7 6 5 4 3 2 1
First Printing

Grow old along with me! The best is yet to be,
The last of life, for which the first was made.

ROBERT BROWNING (1812–1889)

Contents

There is nothing more remarkable in the life of Socrates than that he found time in his old age to learn to dance and play on instruments and thought it time well spent. **MONTAIGNE**

To know how to grow old is the master work of wisdom, and one of the most difficult chapters in the great art of living. **HENRI FRÉDÉRIC AMIEL**

The spiritual eyesight improves as the physical eyesight declines. **PLATO**

Nothing is more dishonorable than an old man, heavy with years, who has no other evidence of having lived long except his age. **SENECA**

If I did not keep telling myself my age over and over again, I am sure I should scarcely be aware of it. Although every day I tell myself, "My poor old fellow, you are seventy," I cannot really persuade myself of it. **ANDRÉ GIDE**

It is always in season for old men to learn. **AESCHYLUS**

Age only matters when one is aging. Now that I have arrived at a great age, I might just as well be twenty. **PABLO PICASSO**

For as I like a young man in whom there is something of the old, so I like an old man in whom there is something of the young. **Cicero**

It is day by day that we go forward; today we are as we were yesterday and tomorrow we shall be like ourselves today. So we go on without being aware of it, and this is one of the miracles of Providence that I so love. **Mme. de Sevigny**

Of the five happinesses, wealth, health, long life, the cultivation of virtue, and a natural death, the greatest is long life. **Chinese Proverb**

You must live long in order to see much. **Cervantes**

For age is opportunity, no less than youth itself, though in another dress. And as the evening twilight fades away, the sky is filled with stars, invisible by the day. **Henry W. Longfellow**

Old age, especially an honored old age, has so great authority, that this is of more value than all the pleasures of youth. **Cicero**

Foreword

TO START WITH, two questions: what is a late bloomer and how is such a person to be defined, first in a general sense and then in the particular sense applicable to the purposes of this book? The earliest use of the term appears to have been in education. "Late bloomer" is a metaphor drawn from botany and agreeably hinting at those flowers whose natural function is to bloom late in the season; what is natural we take to be free from any connotation of displeasure or reproof. Teachers use this kindly term to describe students who, having failed during their early years in school to attain the level of success thought appropriate to them, gradually achieve that level as they proceed upward from one class to the next.

The point to be noted is not that the students were exceptionally gifted and therefore exceptionally disappointing, but only that they were doing less well than they ought to have done. "Ought" is an intimidating word and haunts the strivings of our childhood and youth. It establishes goals that for many of us may prove beyond our reach. Still, if we take care to banish "ought" from our minds, we perceive that to be a late bloomer may be a good thing instead of a bad one. The difficulty of a task heightens the joy of its accomplishment as well as, in some cases, the value of the thing accomplished. Quite rightly, the teacher of a slow student places an emphasis upon his blooming rather than upon his lateness.

As far as this book is concerned, the lateness is every bit as significant as the blooming. Moreover, the lateness isn't merely a consequence of the inevitable passage of years and decades. Rather, it has to do with the moment in time at which we discover, whether through an event dictated by forces outside ourselves or by a seemingly spontaneous personal insight, some worthy means of fulfilling ourselves. The age at which we make this discovery is an irrelevance. In the following pages are late bloomers in their forties and fifties, others in their seventies and eighties. And this is because the process of growing up, like the process of growing old, is various and unpredictable. Some people in their forties have already put on the habits and habiliments of age; other people in their eighties are invincibly young and, like Lewis Carroll's prankish Father William, persist in merrily standing on their heads.

Who are the late bloomers? They are people who at whatever cost and under whatever circumstances have succeeded in finding themselves. Yes, but wait— when you think about it, what a curious phrase that is! To find oneself is plainly to have been lost. It is to have been stumbling about in a dark wood and to have encountered there, unexpectedly and yet how welcomely, a second self, capable of leading one out into the safety of a sunny upland meadow. It is certainly a magical feat and nevertheless one that we observe occurring constantly in real life: a feat that the late bloomers who have been assembled here have manifested by their remarkable lives and that the rest of us do well to admire and draw encouragement from. For we, too, at different stages of the same journey, have our dark woods to traverse and our sunny meadows to attain. If the hour happens to be later than we may have wished, take heart! So much more to be cherished is the bloom.

Late Bloomers

Harry S. Truman · 1884-1972

IT IS A COMMONPLACE to say of Harry S. Truman that few men have ever been less prepared to assume the duties of president of the United States. No vice president under Franklin Delano Roosevelt would have been encouraged to share official responsibilities with him, but Truman had a further disadvantage: he was a comparative stranger to FDR, who had discarded Truman's immediate predecessor in office, Henry A. Wallace, because his political advisers had said Wallace was too radical and would prove a handicap when FDR ran for an unprecedented fourth term.

Senator Truman of Missouri was the product of the Democratic party machine in Kansas City, and his early life had been marked by a series of failures, from farming to selling haberdashery. Little was expected of him when, at the age of sixty, he succeeded FDR. To the general surprise, Truman proved to be a tough-minded executive, who quickly made his weight felt in foreign affairs: he approved the dropping of the atomic bombs on Hiroshima and Nagasaki; he sponsored the Marshall Plan in Europe; and he dismissed General MacArthur at the height of the Korean War. He ran for president in his own right in 1948, against the seemingly far more popular Republican candidate, Thomas E. Dewey, and defeated him. Two of his favorite remarks were "The buck stops here" and "If you can't stand the heat, stay out of the kitchen." He declined to run in 1952, retiring to his home in Independence, Missouri, and becoming in his seventies and eighties one of the most respected and best-loved public figures of his time.

Coco Chanel · 1 8 8 3 ? – 1 9 7 1

SOME PEOPLE ARE FORTUNATE enough to bloom both early and late, with an interval of contented dormancy in between. This was the case with the pioneering dress designer Gabrielle Chanel, universally known as "Coco." Her birthdate is followed by a question mark because nobody knows for certain when she was born; she may well have been past ninety at the time of her death. It appears that there was scarcely a moment in all those years, from an early and impoverished orphanhood in working-class Paris onward into the possession of an immense fortune and world fame, that she was not fiercely in charge of her destiny.

Chanel's first employment was as a milliner, working for an elder sister. By 1912, she had saved enough money to open a modest shop of her own. After the First World War, she moved to grander quarters on the Rue du Cambon, and it was there in the 1920s and early 30s that she became preeminent in the world of haute couture by freeing women from the uncomfortable restraint of corsets and other heavy undergarments and providing them with the exquisitely simple "Chanel look." She designed her first chemise dress in 1920; a few years later came her first collarless cardigan and the celebrated "little black dress" that has remained a classic to this day.

Chanel retired in 1938 and devoted herself to play among the fashionable international set. In 1954 she emerged from retirement and enjoyed an unexpected triumph with designs very similar to those that had startled Paris some thirty years earlier. In a Broadway musical based on Coco's career, Katherine Hepburn, with her usual fearless rigor, portrayed Coco as a tyrant, but one whom an army of women was humbly grateful to be dressed by—not the worst way to stride, head high and without compromise, into history.

Paul Cézanne · 1 8 3 9 – 1 9 0 6

THERE ARE GENIUSES, Mozart and Shelley among them, who make works of art with the seeming ease of a bird in flight, and there are other geniuses—Beethoven and Flaubert will serve as examples—who hammer out their great works by dint of prodigious effort. Of the latter species of genius, Paul Cézanne is notable. All his life, he wrestled with the art of painting as if it were an implacable adversary. It is a pleasant coincidence that the victory he achieved at last was embodied not least nobly in his many representations of a local Provençal landmark, Mont-St.-Victoire.

Cézanne was born in Aix, son of a hatter turned banker, who hoped that his son would continue to advance the family fortunes. Not so; the son took care to fail at banking, and the father let him go off to Paris to paint. And at that occupation, too, despite arduous efforts, he failed—year after year, he submitted pictures to the annual Salons and was rejected. From an older contemporary, Pissarro, he learned the Impressionists' way of painting light, which had for him too ready an air of improvisation. Back to Aix he went, settling down on his father's death in the family home and consenting to begin, however austerely, a family of his own.

Thanks to an inherited income, his failure to sell his work mattered little. He labored on, gradually achieving the goal not of imitating nature but of setting down on canvas an abstracted reconstruction of nature—a reality that was optically both true and false and in terms of his aesthetics entirely true. Toward the end of his life, Cézanne was "discovered" and began to be made much of. To a friend, he wrote, "I have made some progress, but why so belatedly and why so painfully?" Two years before his death, he was given a triumphant retrospective exhibition in Paris, and for the first time he tasted, surely for once with happiness, the wine of fame.

Richard Buckminster Fuller · 1 8 9 5 – 1 9 8 3

A TINY MAN with a big Roman head, R. Buckminster Fuller manifested throughout the first few decades of his life what he and his family regarded as a natural bent for failure—failure first in school and then in several business ventures. Only in his fifties did he become recognized as one of the world's leading inventors, engineers, and educators, comparable in the eyes of his admirers to Leonardo da Vinci.

His major invention was the geodesic dome—a system of interlocking triangles that encloses the maximum volume of space with the least amount of material. These domes are now a familiar sight throughout the world. Metaphorically, they express what Fuller hoped to establish as the guiding principle of mankind: to do more with less in order that people everywhere should have enough of everything. That was the aim of some of his earlier, unsuccessful inventions: the streamlined, three-wheeled Dymaxion car, the prefabricated one-piece steel Dymaxion bathroom, and the mast-supported, spherical Dymaxion house. (Fuller coined the word "Dymaxion" from "dynamic," "maximum," and the suffix "ion.")

In the so-called counterculture of the sixties and seventies, Fuller unexpectedly found himself a hero to the young; his books sold by the hundreds of thousands, and he was much in demand as a speaker. The older he grew, the more he seemed to defy the second law of thermodynamics by gaining energy in the course of expending it. He would speak at Ciceronian length, hour after hour, and once at a public gathering had to be lifted bodily off the stage in order to permit other speakers their rightful turns. Not in the least offended, Fuller continued his discourse to an audience of stagehands, who, like everyone who ever came into his presence, found him well worth listening to.

André Kertész · 1894–1985

NOW GENERALLY CONSIDERED TO BE among the greatest photographers of the twentieth century, André Kertész languished for many years in comparative obscurity in New York City, producing commercial work for *House and Garden* and other magazines and depending largely upon his wife, a successful businesswoman, for financial support. Born in Budapest, he had moved to Paris after the First World War and earned a reputation there as a news photographer. (In later years, he often complained—he was a born complainer, of remarkable range and energy—that Cartier-Bresson, Brassaï, and other widely celebrated photographers had been but callow and untalented imitators of his handiwork.)

Coming to New York in 1939 for what was intended to be a brief visit, the Kertészes were prevented by the threat of war and then by the long war itself from returning to Europe; uneasily they found a perch for themselves in an alien land. In fact, the perch was an exceptionally enviable one—an apartment that hung high above Washington Square Park and from whose open balcony Kertész began to photograph at all seasons and in all weathers the ordinary life of the park. Little noticed by the world, he produced a body of exquisite work that has served to bestow immortality upon a squirrel leaping from benchtop to benchtop, an old man crumpled in sleep against a tree, a girl and boy passing hand in hand through the Washington Arch. And so fame came to him at last. In his eighties, still defiantly complaining that he lacked the attention he deserved, he found himself surrounded by admirers, whose words of praise he accepted with his usual lack of grace. What a crosspatch of a man he was, and how superb an artist!

Julia Child · BORN 1912

THE TRUTH OF THE MAXIM "timing is everything" is demonstrated by people who make their mark by means of an invention that they are ideally suited to and that didn't come into existence until after they were born. Julia Child is a highly successful performer on TV—a method of instructing and entertaining vast numbers of people that was undreamed of when she entered the world, in Pasadena, California, in the summer of 1912. Child's cookbooks have long been deserved best-sellers, but she is especially cherished as a presence on TV: tall, stout, imperturbable in the face of unlooked-for culinary accidents, and with a hint in her well-bred voice and manner of a just barely concealed clownishness.

Julia McWilliams was one of three siblings, of whom their mother used to boast, "I have produced eighteen feet of children." She graduated from Smith College in 1934 and worked at various jobs until, at the outbreak of the Second World War, she joined the O.S.S. in hopes of becoming a spy. In actuality, she served as a file clerk in Washington, D.C., and in the South Pacific, where she met her future husband, Paul Cushing Child. An artist who had become a mapmaker for the O.S.S., Child decided after the war—and after marrying Julia—to join the Foreign Service, which sent him off to Paris. In the course of the six years that the Childs spent in Paris, Julia attended the famous Cordon Bleu cooking school, met the superb chefs Simone Beck and Louisette Bertholle, and agreed to join them in founding a school, L'École des Trois Gourmandes, and in writing a cookbook, published in the United States in 1961 under the title, *Mastering the Art of French Cooking.* It was instantly hailed as a masterpiece. Soon thereafter, already in her fifties, she whipped up her first omelette on TV and the world became her oyster.

Eubie Blake • 1 8 8 3 - 1 9 8 3

THERE ARE PEOPLE WHO BLOOM EARLY, disappear from public view for a long period of time, and then appear again, all the more to be admired because a new generation finds in them certain qualities that were thought to have been lost forever. A double bloomer of this sort was the composer and pianist Eubie Blake, who with his partner Noble Sissle performed successfully in vaudeville for many years and then jointly created the first black musical ever to play on Broadway. It was called *Shuffle Along*, and it became one of the big hits of the early 1920s. Blake and Sissle wrote the scores of several other musicals, none of which proved as popular as their first. Blake's kind of music—ragtime—went out of fashion, and it wasn't until the seventies, with a revival of interest in the early days of jazz, that he returned to prominence. The music of Sissle and Blake was again to be heard on Broadway in *Doctor Jazz, Bubbling Brown Sugar,* and *Eubie.* Blake was then in his eighties, but exceptionally spry and as eager as ever to strut his stuff. Slender to the point of emaciation, he had long skeletal arms and extremely large hands. Entering his nineties, he announced with an air of amused bewilderment, "If I'd known I was going to live this long, I'd have taken better care of myself." Be that as it may, at ninety-five he played piano on the lawn of the White House, celebrating the twenty-fifth anniversary of the Newport Jazz Festival. He lived on to reach the century mark: a happy old man crouched above the keys, playing his own irresistibly appealing music.

Zachary Taylor · 1784-1850

THE TWELFTH PRESIDENT of the United States was a gruff and stubborn army general named Zachary Taylor, who on being elected to the presidency in his sixties had only the sketchiest idea of what was expected of him. He died after a short time in office, of a sickness brought on in part by overexertion at ceremonies in dedication of the Washington Monument, on July 4, 1850, and in part by his distress over allegations of corruption in his administration.

Taylor was a simple, honest soldier, and he found the skullduggery of Washington, D.C., highly distasteful. He had spent most of his professional career in the field, gaining great popular acclaim during the Mexican War by victories achieved at Monterrey and Buena Vista. Known by then as "Old Rough and Ready," he was perceived by Whig politicians to be an ideal candidate for the presidency, and in the Whig convention of 1848 he secured the nomination on the fourth ballot, defeating such distinguished runners-up as Henry Clay, Daniel Webster, and General Winfield Scott.

On becoming president, he continued to act with his usual blunt military forthrightness. He was eager to see California, formerly a Mexican province, admitted to the Union, and when Southern leaders in Congress protested, on the grounds that California's proposed state charter prohibited slavery, "Old Rough and Ready," although himself a slaveholder, let it be known that unless he got his way he would take to the field again and hang anyone who disagreed with him. The seriousness of his threat was not to be doubted, and soon thereafter California entered the Union as the thirty-first state.

Barbara Woodhouse · 1910 – 1988

INFINITE IS THE VARIETY of occupations in which people can achieve success and even, with luck, a measure of fame, and for Barbara Woodhouse it was her knack for training dogs that led to a professional career—one that culminated in a popular television program both in the United Kingdom and the United States, and a number of best-selling books. "Life for me began at seventy," she said, when speaking of her unexpected popularity on TV.

In 1982 *The Guinness Book of Records* credited her with being the world's fastest dog trainer: over a period of thirty-one years she taught 17,136 dogs to obey basic commands (walk, heel, sit, stay, and come). Once, at a demonstration of her prowess in Denver, Colorado, she trained eighty dogs in a single day. Among her sayings: "I can train any dog in five minutes. It's training the owners that takes longer." And to onlookers it often appeared that it was the spirit of the dog owner and not of the dog that she intended to break.

Woodhouse was born Barbara Blackburn in County Dublin, Ireland, where her father was headmaster of a local school. On his early death, his widow moved with her children to Oxford, England, where she raised dogs to earn a living. If a dog appeared troubled, the young Barbara would lead it aside and talk to it in what she called her "little" voice, prompting the animal to take a turn for the better. With horses, she learned to make friends by breathing down her nose at them, which she said was how horses habitually make one another's acquaintance. She considered German shepherds, poodles, and Great Danes the easiest dogs to train and terriers the most difficult. She admired pigs and spiders, and at one time kept a pet spider on her lap while she was watching TV.

Isaac Bashevis Singer ·

THERE IS A GREEK COFFEE SHOP in the West Forties, in New York City, called the Red Flame. It is almost next door to the Algonquin Hotel, with its innumerable literary memories, but the Red Flame is scarcely more than it appears to be, a place for businesspeople in the neighborhood to bolt a quick breakfast or lunch and hasten on to their jobs. Still, the Red Flame is not without a certain bookish flavor, because *The New Yorker* is nearby, and to contributors and members of its staff the coffee shop is an indispensable resource.

One of the patrons of the Red Flame was the writer Isaac Bashevis Singer, who could often be seen seated at a booth just inside the shop's big front windows, looking over a manuscript that, brought down into midtown from his residence on the Upper West Side, he was about to submit to the magazine.

A plump, pink-cheeked, blue-eyed old man, Singer looked like a Jewish Santa Claus. But if his amiable countenance—he smiled as readily at strangers as friends —was an accurate manifestation of his nature, it had little to do with the nature of his writing, which despite its surface humor was filled with darkness. His tales led readers back through centuries of ghetto culture and its accompanying persecutions and survivals into the very heart of some ineradicable evil—to Cain and not Abel. Singer was born in Poland and was expected to follow the family's rabbinic tradition, but he chose instead to become a writer. He emigrated to New York in the 1930s and went to work on the *Daily Forward*, the city's most important Yiddish newspaper. Singer was in his fifties when he began to be recognized by a wide audience. Fame was pleasing to him, but unnecessary. He had lived a long life equably, and his gift had never failed him.

Ed Sullivan • 1 9 0 2 – 1 9 7 4

THERE ARE LATE BLOOMERS whose careers are worth recording as examples of the victory that lucky timing may sometimes achieve over talent—put another way, as examples of how a total absence of talent under certain circumstances can itself amount to a talent. This was the case with Ed Sullivan, a former sportswriter turned tabloid gossip columnist, who in the infancy of television entertainment put together a variety show that for many years dominated the field. Sullivan had gained his fitness for this role as master of ceremonies at benefit shows for soldiers during the Second World War and at an annual Harvest Ball sponsored by his employer, the New York *Daily News.*

Unprepossessing in appearance, Sullivan was a stocky, prognathous man with hunched shoulders, deep-set eyes, and curly, well-greased hair. Lacking any natural grace, he stood motionless onstage, hands linked in front of him, swaying grimly from side to side as, with a dolorous expression, he announced the remarkable performers who made up each cast of *The Ed Sullivan Show* (which he unaccountably came close to pronouncing "shoo"). He must be given credit for launching on national TV Elvis Presley and the Beatles, and for having added to the reputations of such gifted performers as Bob Hope, Ethel Waters, and Victor Borge.

Sullivan became so famous in his own right for lacking star quality that scarcely a single stand-up nightclub comedian in the country failed to bring off a convincing impersonation of him, even on his own show. And to this mockery the accidental impresario gravely consented, baring his big teeth in an uneasy smile.

Charles Darwin · 1 8 0 9 – 1 8 8 2

THE BRITISH SCIENTIST CHARLES DARWIN is a classic example of someone arriving
late at a goal set early in life. Even in choosing a career, young Charles took his
time: having first studied to become a medical doctor, he wondered whether he
might not prefer to be a clergyman, and with that purpose in mind he entered
Christ's Church, Cambridge. It was there that he decided instead to take up the
study of botany, geology, and biology. Having earned his B.A., he accepted the position of naturalist aboard HMS *Beagle,* then about to set sail for a scientific study
of South American waters. The voyage lasted four years, during which Darwin
accumulated an exceptionally ample stock of knowledge on the flora, fauna, and
geology of the Southern Hemisphere.

On his return to England, Darwin began publishing papers on his discoveries,
married his cousin Emma Wedgwood, and began to address the problem of the
origin of species. He worked out a theory of natural selection, but with characteristic caution was reluctant to publish it. His hand was forced when he received a
letter from a young man named Alfred Russel Wallace, proposing almost exactly
the same theory as Darwin's. Honorably and generously, Darwin gave a public
address in the course of which he read Wallace's letter and a letter of his own, written a year earlier than Wallace's, justly establishing the credit due each of them.

His immense work, *The Origin of Species by Means of Natural Selection,* was
published in 1859 and received mingled praise and condemnation. Eleven years later,
he published *The Descent of Man,* which, in theorizing that man was descended
from a hairy creature related in some fashion to the great apes, prompted a scandal
that resounds in fundamentalist religious circles to this day.

Brooke Astor · BORN 1903

NOVEL-WRITING IS WIDELY ASSUMED to be the province of the young. Hemingway, Fitzgerald, and Mailer, among many others, gained their first fame from novels written in their twenties. As for writing a novel in old age, it is thought to be out of the question. Nevertheless, the noted philanthropist Brooke Astor, now in her nineties, wrote in her late eighties a highly regarded novel, *The Last Blossom on the Plum Tree*. It was her first work of fiction, and she composed it with the same dash and elegance that has always marked her public and private utterances. Brought up as an only child in a family that was socially well connected but without wealth (her father was a professional soldier), the last of her three husbands was Vincent Astor, who upon falling mortally ill decided to put her in charge of the immense charitable foundation he was setting up in his will. "Pookie," he told her, "you are going to have a hell of a lot of fun with the foundation when I am gone."

And so she has—fun and continuous hard work, in the course of distributing a total of $140 million to a variety of worthy causes in New York City. Sometimes she pretends to fear that in helping to preserve many local monuments she has herself become a monument. "Not that I would really mind that," she says. "I have seen too much and done too much not to be content with my lot. 'Don't die guessing,' my mother cautioned me, and I hearkened to her words. I will not die guessing. I have led a full life." Upon which she laughs aloud—the quick, spontaneous laugh of a person who has secrets that are still worth keeping.

Colonel Harland Sanders · 1 8 9 0 – 1 9 8 0

ONE OF THE MOST ENTERTAINING rags-to-riches stories of the period after the Second World War was that of Kentucky Colonel Harland Sanders, who in his sixties founded a business—Colonel Sanders' Kentucky Fried Chicken—that unexpectedly took America and much of the world by storm. The Colonel's triumph was all the more remarkable because it occurred at the very moment when professional nutritionists were beginning to argue that fried foods were highly injurious to human beings, an argument that the hot-tempered Colonel rejected as the handiwork of the devil.

As the public embodiment of his succulent brainchild, the white-suited and goateed old Colonel, who was neither an authentic colonel nor a Kentuckian and whose Southern accent and Southern mannerisms markedly increased with the years, was skilled to a degree matched by few businessmen. He had been born on a farm in Indiana and claimed to have learned to cook at his widowed mother's knee. Poverty obliged him to drop out of school in the seventh grade, and in the hardscrabble years that followed he worked, so he liked to boast, as a farmhand, buggy painter, streetcar conductor, ferryboat operator, and life insurance salesman. He acquired a doubtful law degree by means of a correspondence course and practiced doubtful law in Arkansas. Some time later, he opened a filling station in Kentucky, with a quick-order restaurant on the side. The restaurant flourished, serving as its specialty the Colonel's pressure-cooked fried chicken. Having hit on the notion of franchising this culinary crown jewel, he set off on travels that continued unbrokenly into his eighties, preaching from coast to coast the gospel of "finger-lickin' " goodness and turning himself into a crotchety, right-wing, anti-welfare, hell-and-damnation millionaire.

Karen Blixen • 1885-1962

IT IS OFTEN THE CASE that women begin their careers as writers far later than men, having been obliged to devote themselves in youth to the management of families or of family enterprises. Karen Dinesen was born into a distinguished Danish family, attended Oxford, studied painting in Paris and Rome, attempted a play and a few stories, and then married her cousin, Baron Bror von Blixen-Finecke. Her family purchased a large coffee plantation for the newlyweds in British East Africa (now Kenya). The marriage was not a success, and following a divorce, in 1921, the Baroness found herself—childless and in ill health—in charge of running the plantation. In the Depression the coffee market collapsed; the Baroness was obliged to sell the plantation, and she returned to her family home on the coast of Denmark, not far from Elsinore, the presumed location of Hamlet's castle.

The Baroness's first book, *Seven Gothic Tales,* became an unexpected best-seller. Written in English in a lofty, mock-heroic prose style, it was full of blood and thunder, and its tiny, frail author rightly took care to sign it with a male pseudonym, Isak Dinesen. Her next book, also a best-seller, was a work of non-fiction called *Out of Africa,* which evoked with affection the life she had led in the East African highlands, with house servants and field hands as her only trusted companions. Several later books met with success, and the Baroness, no longer hiding behind a pseudonym, became a well-known literary figure in New York and London, where, growing ever tinier and more frail, she was said to subsist entirely on a diet of grapes and Champagne.

OVER THE CENTURIES there have been many able but unamiable popes and a few who have been both able and so amiable that, like St. Francis of Assisi, they may be said to have charmed birds out of the trees. Of this pleasing sort was Pope John XXIII, who, when he was elected pontiff at the advanced age of seventy-seven, said with characteristic genial wit, "My bags are packed." It is widely assumed that the College of Cardinals elected him as a stopgap, counting on him to do little of consequence in the few years that were likely to constitute his reign; after his death, the differing factions in the College would seek to agree on some younger, stronger man.

John astonished all the cardinals and dismayed most of them by becoming an active pope instead of a passive one. He issued an encyclical in 1961 that advocated a variety of social reforms and soon thereafter convened the Second Vatican Council, at which he encouraged greater diversity within the church structure, a fostering of the ecumenical movement, and major innovations in the liturgy. Conservatives in the church hierarchy were gravely shocked; radicals tossed their red caps in the air.

A series of successful diplomatic missions throughout his career had taught John to feel very much at home in the world. In 1953 he was made a cardinal and patriarch of Venice. An episode that illustrates his humor and his diplomacy: at an audience held at the Vatican and attended by several hundred journalists, John said, "There are ten commandments. Now, you are journalists and for you there is but a single paramount commandment: 'Thou shalt not bear false witness.' As for the other nine . . ." Whereupon the Pope shrugged his shoulders and extended his arms in the age-old Mediterranean gesture for indifference. He chuckled as the enchanted recipients of this playful papal injunction hastened out of the audience chamber.

Alice Hamilton • 1 8 6 9 – 1 9 7 0

LIKE HER ELDER SISTER EDITH (see page 80), Alice Hamilton grew up in the shadow of a dominating father and at his insistence attended Miss Porter's Finishing School for Young Ladies, in Farmington, Connecticut. Unwilling to accept the usual strict Victorian limits on how female members of "nice" American families were supposed to behave, she went on to college and medical school and for over a decade worked closely with her friend Jane Addams, the well-known social reformer and founder of Hull House, a settlement house in the Chicago slums. Hamilton's medical specialty was the study of the diseases workers in factories were then commonly faced with in the course of carrying out their daily tasks. She engaged in many battles for improved industrial safety standards, especially in respect to lead poisoning, on which she came to be recognized as one of the world's leading authorities. Eventually she became a special investigator for the United States Bureau of Labor and was appointed by Harvard University to be its first professor of public health. Hamilton published hundreds of papers on industrial toxology and ended by writing an autobiography in which she attacked conventional shibboleths with her usual vigor. She lived to be a hundred, to the end championing public health and personal liberty. Like her sister, she was a lesbian, and that, too, was for her—as it had never been for Edith—a cause worth fighting for. In her youth, she dressed in mannish clothing, wore her hair cropped short, and strode about like a heavyweight boxer in top fighting trim. Zestfully, she seemed to be saying that if the world didn't approve of her conduct, so much the worse for the world.

Edward Hopper • 1 8 8 2 – 1 9 6 7

EDWARD HOPPER WAS a big, hulking, solemn-faced man, who took care to keep the world at a distance, especially when the world, bewitched by his paintings, sought to impute to them a sociological content. Hopper is one of the most popular of American painters, rivaling Maxfield Parrish and Norman Rockwell in that respect. This rivalry would have aroused contempt in him for those who called attention to it, all the more if they dared to see in it a puzzle—Parrish and Rockwell so sunny in their choice of subject matter, Hopper so dour. The quality of the work of art and not its subject matter is what concerns the artist, and Hopper denied that his dark streets, his all-night diners, his bleak white houses facing an empty sea expressed loneliness or any other conventional emotion. What he painted was not the American scene but himself, and the less said about himself the better.

Hopper may have adopted this curmudgeonly facade during the years when, failing to earn a living as a "serious" artist, he was obliged to devote himself to commercial illustration. Born in Nyack, New York, of a family long settled in the neighborhood, he had begun his artistic studies under the tutelage of Robert Henri, a member of the so-called Ashcan school of American art. Hopper believed in the methods of the school but not in their purposes, and three early visits to Paris left him similarly detached from the radical aesthetic experiments under way there. Hopper was well into his sixties when substantial recognition arrived—too late, he might have said, to do him any harm.

Edward $\mathcal{VII}$ • 1 8 4 1 – 1 9 1 0

TO BE YOUNG, intelligent, energetic, and eager to serve one's country and then to be kept waiting until one is old, ill, and fearful of taking any strong action has the ring of a scary ancient folktale in which an unscrupulous witch casts a spell over somebody of whom she disapproves. This sorry fate can also befall one in real life, as the biography of Edward VII, King of Great Britain and Ireland, vividly reveals. He was the firstborn son of Queen Victoria and the Prince Consort, and his mother played the role not of an unscrupulous witch but, still worse, of a scrupulous one. His parents had strict notions of how Edward should be educated and comport himself as a royal personage; being a sociable young man, he was always getting into scrapes, and during a summer vacation from his studies at Cambridge he served with the Grenadier guards in Ireland.

In Victoria's opinion, word of his obstreperous behavior in Dublin darkened the last days of the Prince Consort. From that moment on, she refused to grant him any part in matters of importance, whether at home or at court. Displaying admirable patience in public, in private Edward took revenge on his mother by filling his otherwise idle days with sports, travel, and sexual dalliance—in short, conduct the opposite of Victoria's sour, unsmiling pursuit of duty. The contest between mother and son was a protracted and unequal one. The Widow of Windsor achieved the longest reign of any monarch in British history—sixty-four years— and on succeeding her, Edward had but a short time to live. An earlier illness of his prompted from the poet laureate of England, Alfred Austen, two of the worst lines of poetry ever penned: "Across the wires the electric message came / 'He is no better, he is much the same.'"

Louise Nevelson · 1 8 9 9 – 1 9 8 8

THE SCULPTOR LOUISE NEVELSON achieved a deserved public success in her sixties. She was born in Kiev, Russia, one of four children of Isaac and Minna Berliawsky. The family emigrated to the United States in 1905, settling in Rockland, Maine, where the father became a prosperous builder and where Louise attended the public schools. At an early age, Louise and her three siblings all manifested a remarkable gift for drawing. On reaching eighteen, Louise married a wealthy young New York businessman, by whom she had a child. Becoming dissatisfied with marriage and motherhood, she obtained a divorce and, armed with prodigious energy and a dominating physical presence, set about testing her talents in a number of fields— singing, dancing, and acting, as well as painting and sculpture.

It took her many years to turn from painting to sculpture and then to find her way to her particular form of it: constructions of black-painted wood that make use of bits and pieces of abandoned chairs, fruit crates, and other debris and that convey a sense of benign mystery. After an extended period of obscurity, in the 1950s Nevelson's works began to be exhibited and purchased by influential museums and collectors. Almost at once, she created the sensation that she had long been ready for and that she enjoyed for many years in her big old studio building in SoHo, amid her carefully tended rooftop roses and the heaps of junk out of which she fashioned her haunting art.

Thelonious Monk •

EARLY SUCCESS IN THE ARTS has its dangers, but to work hard and go for years without public recognition is also productive of dangers, not least a bitterness that, in Yeats's phrase, makes a stone of the heart. Thelonious Monk, though always admired by a small number of his fellow jazz musicians, endured prolonged public neglect, in the face of which he remained without rancor, following his bent. As if he and his piano were equals setting out together on an unprecedented journey, they explored possibilities in sound—dissonance, alteration in tempo, bizarre chords—that left the world astonished. When the world at last caught up with Monk, nothing changed; he was quoted as saying that all he had ever done was try to use notes differently, and whatever he meant by "differently," it had proved to be enough.

Monk was born in North Carolina and moved to New York City with his mother and two siblings when he was four years old. He was playing the piano by ear at six, reading music at eight, and improvising in local bands at thirteen. At sixteen he dropped out of high school to tour the country with a band whose purpose was to help draw crowds for an itinerant evangelist preacher. Back in New York, young Monk played with a variety of bands in Harlem, joining forces with Charlie Parker, Dizzy Gillespie, Kenny Clarke, and Charlie Christian to invent the species of jazz known as bebop. (According to a Monk biographer, Monk said, "I was calling it bip-bop, but the others must have heard me wrong.") His fellow inventors proceeded to become stars, but during the obscurity and hard times of the next two decades Monk continued to use notes in the way that he had always heard them, and these notes became some of his most cherished compositions: "Blue Monk," "Bemsha Swing," and "Little Rootie Tootie." Fame came at last—best-selling record albums, his face on the cover of *Time*, and, in 1976, a public performance in Carnegie Hall.

THE USUAL VIEW OF nineteenth-century New Englanders as being austere and over-cautious is the stuff of legend; in fact, New England in that epoch was alive with uncounted hundreds of cranks continuously founding cults based upon mesmerism, spiritualism, phrenology, hydropathy, homeopathy, and other manifestations of false science. A major purpose of these popular movements was the attainment of perfect physical and mental health—a goal generally linked to a variety of religious beliefs based on the Bible. Jesus had healed the sick by a laying on of hands, and many itinerant "manipulists" (commonly bestowing on themselves the title of "Doctor") claimed to be following in his footsteps.

One noted mental healer of the day, Dr. Phineas Parkhurst Quimby, having abandoned mesmerism, developed a method of curing ill health that he defined as Christian Science. Among his disciples was a middle-aged woman of sickly con-stitution and contentious disposition, who on breaking with Quimby and estab-lishing her own version of Christian Science was soon to become famous in her own right. Like Quimby, Mary Baker Eddy held that disease was a mental misstep, death an aberration, the practice of medicine quackery. In the course of time, she added a refinement to her basic doctrines: something that she identified as Malicious Animal Magnetism (M.A.M., for short) could send forth destructive streams of telepathic influence from one mind to another. Eddy was a charismatic teacher and a prolific writer. Her principles were contained in a voluminous work, *Science and Health,* which she constantly altered as her notions grew more complex and her sect prospered; it had gone through 382 editions by the time of Eddy's death, unexpected and unwelcome at eighty-nine.

Wilbur Lucius Cross • 1862-1948

AN INTERESTING CATEGORY of late bloomers consists of people who, having earned distinction in a lifetime of labor in one field, achieve in old age a career of equal distinction in another and altogether different field. Such a person was Wilbur Lucius Cross, who liked to boast of being a Connecticut Yankee—his family settled in the pioneering river town of Wethersfield in 1637—and who spent most of his life in the groves of academe, rising in the hierarchy of Yale University faculty to the post of dean of the graduate school. He became a leading authority on the development of the English novel and the author of a biography of Laurence Sterne, whose comic and bawdy tale *The Life and Times of Tristram Shandy,* Cross rescued from the neglect into which it had fallen in prim Victorian times.

In 1930 Cross reached the mandatory retirement age of sixty-eight and stepped at once from the supposed peace and quiet of the Yale campus into the Donnybrook of politics. He accepted the nomination for governor of the state from the Democratic Party, then accustomed to years of overwhelming defeat. Cross campaigned vigorously from small town to small town, swapping stories in the vernacular mode familiar to him from childhood. To widespread astonishment, he won the election by a substantial margin and served successfully for three terms, again and again outmaneuvering the Republican-dominated legislature in order to accomplish his goals. Cross's mastery of political strategies puzzled those among his adversaries who were unaware that the politics practiced in academia is every bit as bloodthirsty as that to be found in the outside world.

Michel de Montaigne · 1533-1592

IF ONE WERE TO TAKE A POLL asking scholars throughout the world to name the *nicest* person in history, the winner would almost certainly be Michel de Montaigne. Nor would the list of runners-up be very long, history consisting of innumerable villains and a few heroes, and of those heroes a large number being grim and distant —not the sort one would choose to eat, drink, and be merry with. Montaigne is the grand exception: charming, kindly, generous, learned, and uncomplaining under stress. His father, apparently every bit as nice as he was, though without his literary talent, built up the family fortune and made possible the life of cultivated ease Montaigne led in his chateau among the vineyards in the Bordelaise countryside.

In his forties (and thinking himself to be already well advanced in age) he sat down to write in a form he invented as he went along. That was why he called the stout volumes that contained them *Essais*—that is, in English, "tentative efforts, experiments." And what experiments they were, never to be surpassed for breadth of knowledge, honesty of feeling, and seductiveness of style.

"It is myself that I portray," Montaigne says in a preliminary note to the reader, slyly going on to suggest that it will be unreasonable for us to spend our leisure "on so frivolous and vain a subject." In truth, his ruminations, at once merry and serious, encourage us to prize tranquillity, to subdue pride—"There is no use our mounting on stilts, for on stilts we must still walk on our own legs"— and not to dread an end that we share with everything in nature.

Cathleen Nesbitt · 1889 - 1982

ACTRESSES ARE LIKELY TO BLOOM EARLY, but always at the risk of dropping out of sight for a considerable period and of being greeted on their return to the stage as late bloomers, by audiences of a generation that has never known them. How valorous actresses must be at such a moment, when with the advantage of a youthful freshness no longer theirs they speak the lines that will bring them success or failure! In either case, once the performance is over, with a practiced radiance they must bow and smile, bow and smile, until the curtain falls. Cathleen Nesbitt was fortunate enough to bloom both early and late—so late, indeed, that she was still enchanting audiences in her tenth decade.

Born in England, in her first youth and beauty Nesbitt made her debut on the London stage in 1910. Her American debut the following year was in an Abbey Theatre production of *The Well of the Saints.* In the years before the First World War she gained a reputation for sexual daring as the mistress of the handsome poet Rupert Brooke—naked they swam in the streams outside Grantchester, to the alarm of their tweedy Edwardian neighbors. After the war (in which Brooke died), Nesbitt became one of the most successful actresses on the British stage. She co-starred with Tallulah Bankhead and Herbert Marshall in *This Marriage,* during the run of which Nesbitt, by then herself married, enlivened matters by nursing her baby backstage. In her sixties, she returned to New York in T. S. Eliot's *The Cocktail Party,* followed by *Gigi, Sabrina Fair,* and *My Fair Lady.* She was playing Mrs. Higgins with irresistible snooty charm in a revival of *My Fair Lady* a year before she died, at ninety-four.

Joseph Conrad · 1 8 5 7 - 1 9 2 4

WHEN, AT A LITERARY GATHERING, the discussion turns to the difficulty of writing well in a language not one's own, a writer certain to be mentioned is Joseph Conrad. Born in Poland, he received at baptism the burden of the names Josef Teodor Konrad Nalecz Korzeniowski. Upon abandoning a long and successful career as a ship's officer and adopting a new career as an author, he prudently whittled his name down to four simple syllables, which readers of novels have found easy to pronounce and remember. Conrad's father, a writer and political activist, was sent into exile when Conrad was a child. By the time Conrad had reached adolescence, both his parents were dead. In 1874, hoping to escape the harshness of life in Russian Poland by going to sea, he journeyed to Marseilles and entered the French merchant service, switching over a few years later into its British equivalent. In 1886 he became a British subject, and after many voyages to what were then thought of as the outposts of civilization—Singapore, Borneo, the Belgian Congo—he undertook to transform some of the hard facts of his career into fiction.

His first novel, *Almayer's Folly,* was published in 1895 and, having been well received, prompted the middle-aged Conrad to give up the sea in favor of a proper British author's life, which in his case came to include a cottage in Kent, a wife, two sons, and a nearby circle of fellow novelists eager to offer encouragement. In an elegant prose style that any native-born speaker of English would envy, one after another Conrad gouged out his short stories and novels—*The Outcast of the Islands, The Heart of Darkness, Lord Jim.* The narrator he often employs is his double: Marlow, a gentle and wise man, who, having seen much of the world, has many adventures to relate, not alone for the drama they embody but for the moral issues they raise.

Louise Bourgeois · BORN 1911

A SMALL, SOFT-SPOKEN WOMAN, gentle in person but fiery in the nature of her art, Louise Bourgeois was born in Paris, took a degree at the Sorbonne, studied at the Academy of Beaux Arts, and emigrated to the United States in 1938. It wasn't until the 1960s and 1970s that she developed her characteristic and much admired sculptures in stone and bronze, in which anthropomorphic shapes give the impression that some sort of desperate struggle is taking place within a single contorted and deformed body, or perhaps between two or more such bodies. Critics tend to speak in a gingerly fashion of the phallic content in her work; this gingerliness amuses Bourgeois—she is ready to admit that if one believes the struggle to be sexual, the male participant may be assumed to be losing. To that degree, she resembles the humorist James Thurber, who, a generation earlier than Bourgeois and from the point of view of an intimidated male, depicted in scores of drawings and short prose pieces a titanic and never-ending battle between the sexes. Like many sculptors, the older Bourgeois becomes, the larger the works of art she creates, as if to defy mortality by giving proof of an energy undiminished and an ambition unfulfilled.

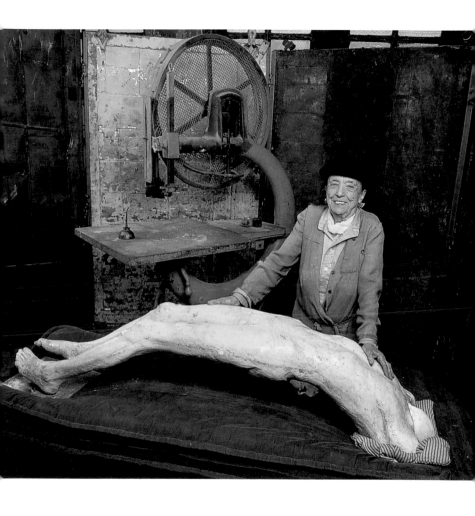

Philip Johnson · BORN 1906

AN OBVIOUS ADVANTAGE to being rich is that it permits a late start in choosing the career best suited to one's talents. The architect Philip Johnson is a case in point. Born in 1906, in Cleveland, Ohio, he was the scion of a family prominent in the affairs of that city, and there was never any doubt that young Philip was free to do whatever he pleased with his life. It is a precept that Johnson continues to embrace today, at ninety, with unabated eccentric high spirits. Having graduated from Harvard, he was invited by his friend Alfred Barr, head of the newly founded Museum of Modern Art, in New York City, to help organize at the museum a department of architecture and design—at the time an unheard-of novelty. With another friend, the architectural historian Henry-Russell Hitchcock, in 1932 Johnson put on an exhibition of contemporary architecture for which he and Hitchcock coined the term "International style."

Having come to the conclusion that he would rather be a practicing architect than merely a critic of and writer about architecture, Johnson enrolled in the Graduate School of Design at Harvard and, having the means to do so, designed and built for himself as a student project a handsome little house in Cambridge that paid homage to his idol, Mies van der Rohe. He launched his practice in New York City in 1945 and has since designed innumerable skyscraper office buildings, museums, churches, and private houses all over the world. In 1945, on his estate in New Canaan, Connecticut, he designed and built his famous Glass House, also inspired by Mies. The Glass House and a half-dozen other nearby structures designed by Johnson—he has always boasted that he is himself his own best client—are to go on his death to the National Trust for Historic Preservation.

John Cromwell · 1 8 8 7 – 1 9 7 9

THE MOST CELEBRATED OF CROMWELLS was Oliver (1599–1658), a disagreeable man bent on dealing harshly with his adversaries, always in the name of serving God. ("I beseech ye in the bowels of Christ," he wrote on one occasion, "think that ye may be mistaken.") A much later and more agreeable Cromwell was John, who began his professional career as an actor and switched in his middle years to directing plays on Broadway and movies in Hollywood. Several of his movies were of exceptionally high quality; it was fortunate for him that they were also profitable. The most famous of them was *Of Human Bondage,* which starred Leslie Howard and Bette Davis. Others were *The Prisoner of Zenda, Abe Lincoln in Illinois,* and *So Ends Our Night.*

In his eighties, Cromwell returned to the stage. A tall, handsome man, he accommodated himself gracefully to the manner in which his career had circled round to its beginnings. He accepted small roles without complaint, good-humoredly explaining to his fellow actors at the first run-through of a play that it might take him somewhat longer than they to memorize lines but memorize them he would. And so he did, invariably earning excellent reviews. Cromwell attributed his stalwart health to an eccentricity: his midday meal consisted of a quart of buttermilk. Another eccentricity: he was married four times, to four actresses. With the last of them, Ruth Nelson, he often appeared at the Long Wharf Theatre, in New Haven, Connecticut, where audiences counted on seeing them onstage together—it was a poor playwright surely who couldn't cobble up a plot that would provide roles for such a merry old couple.

Imogen Cunningham • 1·8 8 3 – 1 9 7 6

ONE OF THE FIELDS OF ACTIVITY accessible to women when they began, in the late nineteenth century, to escape the conventional petty tyrannies of the household was photography. An art and craft that was a cousin of painting, in which well-brought-up young women had always been encouraged to acquire a certain measure of skill, it had the advantage of being able to be practiced indoors as well as outdoors, among attractive people in respectable circumstances. Moreover, if one didn't wish to soil one's hands in the darkroom, somebody could be hired to carry out the messy, smelly task of developing negatives.

Imogen Cunningham was among the young women who chose to make a career in photography. At eighteen, inspired by the photographs taken by the pioneer American portraitist Gertrude Kaesebier, she set about learning the craft from the bottom up, majoring in chemistry at the University of Washington and upon graduation going to work in Seattle, in the studio of the photographer Edward S. Curtis. She went abroad to study photographic chemistry at a technical school in Dresden and on returning to this country met two of her idols, Kaesebier and Alfred Stieglitz, in New York City, and set up a studio of her own in Seattle.

Cunningham gained fame slowly, winning international attention only in her seventies and eighties. When she began to apply for Guggenheim grants and was repeatedly turned down, with characteristic boldness she flew east, entered the Guggenheim offices, and demonstrated her intellectual and physical vigor by bully-ragging everyone in sight. She received a grant at the age of eighty-seven and was quick to put the money to good use.

Jean-Jacques Rousseau · 1712-1778

JEAN-JACQUES ROUSSEAU had the saddest of starts—his mother died at his birth—and the saddest of ends—he died insane, from a sudden heart attack that was long thought to have been suicide. In the years between he enjoyed a spectacular roller coaster of a life, which after a disorderly youth led to his being regarded in middle age as one of the leading writers of the day. His first fame was earned with an epistolary novel, *La Nouvelle Héloïse,* which argued that family life was the natural ideal of mankind. (Rousseau's practice rarely coincided with his theories; he fathered five children by one of his mistresses and was quick to hand the infants over to a foundling hospital.) His next book was a nonfiction work describing what he called the Social Contract. Its celebrated opening sentence—"Man is born free; and everywhere he is in chains"—retains its puissance to this day. Rousseau coined the phrase "Liberty, Equality, Fraternity," which became the battle cry of the French Revolution. He wrote a second epistolary novel, *Émile,* which dealt with the education of the young, and profoundly influenced such pedagogues as Froebel and Pestalozzi. Having quarreled with everyone who mattered to him in France, Rousseau accepted an invitation from the philosopher David Hume to settle in England. There he composed most of his *Confessions,* which shocked his contemporaries by their exceptional candor and, understandably, sold very well. All too soon, his quarrelsome nature alienated his admirers in England and he returned to France, where, friendless and ill, he was reduced to earning a sorry living as a copyist. Sixteen years after his death, his remains were dug up and entombed in the Pantheon, in Paris.

Romare Bearden • 1 9 1 4 – 1 9 8 8

BORN IN NORTH CAROLINA but moving early to New York City, Romare Bearden was a black man with exceptionally light skin, who was often mistaken for white and would have found it easy enough to "pass," but who vehemently elected not to do so. Indeed, he spent much of his career seeking to make sure black artists were given as ample an opportunity as their white colleagues to have their handiwork exhibited and judged on its merits.

In person, Bearden was big and round, with a bald head and a broad smile, and he made friends wherever he went; when there were parties, Bearden was at the center of them, having a good time. His subject matter was the ordinary daily life of black people. He painted in a calculatedly primitive style, with bold primary colors serving to evoke greeny tropical jungles not unlike those imagined by Henri Rousseau, and with figures drawn in a childlike fashion, as if by means of comic distortion to place us at a protective distance from reality. Bearden appears to be telling us that if life is joyous, it is also hard and sometimes terrible; one longs to embrace it but must remain on guard.

Bearden came late to public recognition—it wasn't until he was in his middle fifties that he was given a one-man show at the Museum of Modern Art, in New York City—but he had learned in youth the first rule in respect to fame and the part it plays in the world of the arts, to wit, that one can put oneself in the posture to be struck by lightning, but lightning may never strike. Meanwhile, eagerly and without bitterness, one goes on working.

Sir Alexander Fleming · 1 8 8 1 – 1 9 5 5

SIR ALEXANDER FLEMING achieved fame in middle age by dint of an accident—one that, as a well-disciplined scientist, he was quick to recognize and take appropriate advantage of. Born in Scotland and educated there and at the medical school of London University, he served with distinction in the First World War and then returned to the university to undertake research into the nature of bacterial infections, a realm of science made prominent by the many deaths incurred by hospitalized men during the war and in the subsequent worldwide influenza epidemic.

In the course of attempting to isolate a substance capable of preventing influenza, Fleming prepared a staphylococcus culture plate, which by chance he left exposed on a windowsill in his laboratory. A day or so later, a friend visiting the laboratory pointed out to Fleming that a mold had developed on the plate and that this mold had created a bacteria-free circle around itself. Fleming at once appreciated the significance of the mold, which he named penicillin and which became the first antibiotic to be used successfully in the treatment of bacterial infections in human beings. For this discovery Fleming was knighted in 1944 and, the following year, shared a Nobel prize with two of his fellow workers, Howard Florey and Ernst Chain.

Edith Hamilton · 1 8 6 7 – 1 9 6 3

THE CLASSICAL SCHOLAR EDITH HAMILTON became celebrated late in life as the author of *The Greek Way,* which interpreted in an easy-to-understand style the ancient Greek concept of how life ought to be led. This best-seller was followed by *The Roman Way,* which enjoyed a similar success. In her nineties Hamilton was still hard at work, examining such diverse literary figures as Corneille, Goethe, and William Faulkner.

Behind the popularity that Hamilton earned in age lay decades of learning and teaching. Member of a family of exceptional intellectual distinction, she was one of five children born to Gertrude and Montgomery Hamilton. Hamilton's father was a rich American from the Middle West, who appears to have devoted his life to the rearing and domination of his children—none of them married until after his death and none had children. Little Edith was reading Greek and Latin by the age of seven. She attended Miss Porter's Finishing School for Young Ladies, in Farmington, Connecticut, where her parents rented a house. Edith and her father were to be seen strolling every evening arm in arm up and down its quiet Main Street. To the dismay of Miss Porter, Edith chose upon graduation not to consider herself "finished" but to attend the recently founded Bryn Mawr College, and after further study abroad she accepted in 1896 appointment as Director of the Bryn Mawr School in Baltimore, Maryland, where she remained until 1922.

Hamilton was not least Greek in being lesbian. For much of her life, her companion was a banker in Washington, D.C., where they shared a house. Summers were spent in Bar Harbor, Maine, and in travel. In 1957, in a ceremony held in the theater of Herodes Atticus, at the foot of the Acropolis, Hamilton was named an honorary citizen of Athens.

Louis I. Kahn · 1901–1974

ARCHITECTURE IS WELL KNOWN TO BE a profession favorable to the old. In it, to be
a late bloomer is not to be late at all; one is right on time. A drawback to this otherwise agreeable situation is that architects have found no way of exceeding the nor-
mal life span. Louis I. Kahn was at the peak of his career as an architect and as a
teacher of architecture when, at seventy-three, he fell dead of a heart attack in
Pennsylvania Station, in New York City. This fatal mishap came as no surprise to
friends—he was always racketing about the world by air, seeking new commissions
and completing old ones, at a rate that would have exhausted a twenty-year-old. His
haste was all the more understandable because he had spent so much of his career
in comparative obscurity. He rejoiced in the fame he had earned and was boyishly
eager to earn still more.

Born in Estonia, Kahn and his family emigrated to Philadelphia in 1905. He
was brought up in the Philadelphia public schools and graduated with a degree in
architecture from the University of Pennsylvania. He first gained a national reputation in 1953, with his design for an addition to the Yale Art Gallery. Many other
much-praised commissions followed: the Salk Institute, in California; the Kimbell
Museum, in Texas; government buildings in Bangladesh. Kahn was influenced by
the monumentality of ancient Roman architecture, especially by the immense
brick arches that are visible to us but that citizens of those times never saw; Roman
architects took pains to hide their bricks behind marble. A tiny man with a face
badly burned in childhood and a stuttery, high-pitched voice, Kahn was nonetheless
irresistible to women. At an exhibition of his work in New York City after his
death, his widow, his legitimate children, his mistresses, and his illegitimate children all gathered in a proud, family-like group to celebrate his greatness.

Daniel Defoe • 1 6 6 0 – 1 7 3 1

IT IS RARE FOR BUSINESSMEN to be writers, still rarer for them to be writers of fiction, and rarest of all—indeed, almost unprecedented—for them to write novels capable of winning a place among the greatest ever written. Daniel Defoe achieved this distinction late in life, after having oscillated continuously between success and failure—between the threat of debtors' prison and the company of kings— in the course of pursuing half a dozen commercial careers.

The son of a butcher, Defoe was married young to a woman who brought him a splendid dowry and bore him seven children. He went into trade, at various times importing and selling hosiery, wine, tobacco, and marine insurance, the latter activity (undertaken in behalf of King William III) causing him to go bankrupt for an immense sum. Throughout much of his life, he served the government as a secret agent and pamphleteer, publishing innumerable articles on political and economic topics as he continued to teeter—seemingly always in good spirits—on the brink of financial ruin.

Nearing sixty, he began to experiment with a new literary form called the novel and within a span of six years composed several classic works that helped to shape the form, including *The Life and Surprizing Adventures of Robinson Crusoe, The Fortunes and Misfortunes of the Famous Moll Flanders,* and *A Journal of the Plague Year.* So precise were his descriptions of scenes and events that most of his readers assumed that they were reading history instead of fiction. Poor Defoe! For all his fame and the popularity of his writings, he died in an alleyway, hiding from the wrath of an importunate creditor.

Harriet Doerr • BORN 1910

HARRIET DOERR IS one of that small company of people who in late middle age turn to writing about the past not to console themselves with memories of a life they have been obliged to leave behind, but to make clear that they continue to respond to the life they see flowing all around them, in which they are determined not to relinquish their earned share. For what a poor thing consolation is, compared to the challenge, as we grow older, of being cuffed and spun about in the turmoil of everyday existence.

It is that challenge which prompted Doerr to write her exquisite best-selling book, *The Stones of Ibarra.* To be sure, its contents rely on the indispensable resources of memory (she and her husband spent most of their lives in a small village in Mexico), but the act of writing it was in answer to a family challenge: with the death of her husband, whom she had dropped out of college to marry, her children dared her to go back to college, earn a degree, and make a career for herself. And she did so, with zest and an ever-increasing skill. At eighty, by then a well-known author and far removed from the conventional gentilities of the Pasadena, California, in which she was born and raised, she had the candor to write, "There's nothing wrong with me that having a man in love with me wouldn't cure."

Leo Castelli ·

SOME ART DEALERS ARE SCHOLARS; others are scoundrels. But no matter what pigeonhole of probity or brigandage they may happen to fall into, one thing is certain—artists tend to disdain them as necessary evils. Marcel Duchamp unkindly called them lice, and other unwelcome epithets abound, in part because the making of art and the selling of art are activities radically at odds with each other. Artists like to do their work without thinking about money, and dealers can afford to think of little else.

During the past thirty or forty years in New York City, one of the few dealers to escape being metaphorically hanged, drawn, and quartered by artists has also been one of the most successful. Leo Castelli, now in his late eighties, is a small, witty, courtly man, wearing exquisite clothes and speaking in an exquisite low voice in any of the five languages he feels at home in. Born in Trieste and growing up with an old-fashioned gentlemanly aversion to business (and acquiring along the way a wealthy father-in-law, who generously underwrote that aversion), Castelli didn't get around to opening an art gallery until he was well into middle age. Once started, he proved to have an exceptional eye and a knack for nourishing beginners. It is hard to imagine an assortment of artists more gifted and more sought after than those Castelli accumulated during the boom years of the seventies and eighties; among them Jasper Johns, Robert Rauschenberg, and Andy Warhol. He helped to make all of them rich and in spite of his best efforts to the contrary, shockingly he made himself rich as well. In marriage, he bloomed early and late: at the age of eighty-eight, he took as his third bride a woman in her thirties, telling the press, "I feel as young as I did the first time I got married, which was a long time ago."

Margaret Fogarty Rudkin · 1 8 9 7 – 1 9 6 7

MARGARET FOGARTY RUDKIN, universally known as Peggy, was a redheaded, effervescent woman of Irish descent, born in modest circumstances in a brownstone in New York City and coming to enjoy with age a mock-Tudor mansion in Connecticut, an ancient manor house in Ireland, and a contemporary house in Florida. In her middle years she found her way to great wealth as a consequence of two unrelated events that had the look of being catastrophes: her husband's financial resources were wiped out by the Depression, and it was discovered that the health of the youngest of her three sons was being endangered by an allergy that made it impossible for him to eat, among other items in his diet, commercially produced bread.

In an abandoned greenhouse on the family estate, Maggie Rudkin started making bread as she remembered her grandmother having made it, with stone-milled flour, honey, molasses, and the like. The bread seemed to improve her son's health, and word of its deliciousness spread among neighbors with whom she shared it. Peggy found herself baking so much bread that she had to take on paid help and sell the bread instead of giving it away. Her husband carried some loaves to a fashionable food shop in New York City, where it readily sold at twice the price of ordinary bread.

Unexpectedly, the Rudkins discovered that they had founded a business. What to call the product? They decided to name it after their estate, Pepperidge Farm. Sales doubled and tripled from one year to the next, and the Rudkins kept on adding new products. In 1960 they sold the business to the Campbell Soup Company for $28 million and went on working.

Boris Karloff · 1887 – 1969

A KINDLY, TEA-DRINKING ENGLISH GENTLEMAN named William Henry Pratt was born in the pleasant London suburb of Dulwich, graduated from London University, emigrated to Canada, acted in a number of touring companies of little reputation, drifted to Hollywood and worked for many years as an extra in dozens of silent films and a few undistinguished talkies, and then, in his forties, suddenly and unexpectedly gained fame and fortune under the name of Boris Karloff, playing the monster in *Frankenstein.* From Pratt's point of view, this triumph was all the more ironic because his handsome, saturnine features were almost totally disguised by the thick, scary makeup he was obliged to wear and because his elegant, English-accented voice was employed only to utter a few animal-like grunts and monosyllables: "Food . . . good, fire . . . bad."

A further irony was that the role of the monster had been turned down by his fellow actor Bela Lugosi, already a big box-office draw as a result of having starred in an earlier movie horror classic, *Dracula.* Inevitably, Hollywood saw that millions were to be made by finding ways of starring both Karloff and Lugosi in a dozen or so movies in the same popular vein. When Karloff wasn't typecast as a monster, he tended to play a mad scientist or some other repellent character as far as possible removed from his chosen way of life off-camera, which included raising funds for needy children and playing cricket with members of the British colony in Hollywood.

Emily Post · 1873 – 1960

EMILY POST, throughout much of her lifetime and, by ghostly descent through members of later generations of her family, has served continuously over several decades as the best-known arbiter of social customs in the United States. She was fitted for this task by birth and upbringing, and she took a disdainful view of anyone who supposed that birth and upbringing were but trifles, which any pushy outsider could bluffly brush aside. In her view, a high standard of etiquette was every bit as necessary to a well-ordered society as laws and religious beliefs; to behave correctly at a dinner party ("No more floating island, thank you. It was delicious") was as much an expression of morality as truth-telling under oath.

Post was born Emily Price, only child of the distinguished New York City architect Bruce Price, whose clients included the first members of "Society" to build cottages in the nearby fashionable resort of Tuxedo Park. She married a banker, from whom, after a couple of children had been born to them, she divorced on the grounds of his conspicuous infidelities. As a renowned society hostess, she was invited in her late fifties to compose a book of etiquette, which was published under the title *Etiquette—The Blue Book of Social Usage.* It was an instant best-seller, which led her to launch a successful syndicated question-and-answer newspaper column and a radio program.

Having become rich and famous, Post divided her time according to season between New York City, Tuxedo Park (in a house her father had designed), Martha's Vineyard, and European travel. Reluctantly, she accommodated her rules of conduct to the slangy, servantless state that the world of her youth had given way to.

Hans Hofmann · 1 8 8 0 – 1 9 6 6

IT IS OFTEN THE CASE with artists that the older they grow, the greater the chances they take—instead of prudently carrying a cane in age, to the general astonishment they begin to dance waltzes. Hans Hofmann was just such an artist, seeming with every year of his life to push harder and harder against the conventional limits determining how one applies paint to canvas. Born in Germany, Hofmann set out on his career as an artist in Paris, where he shared with Matisse, Picasso, and Braque their pioneering forays into Fauvism and Cubism. The First World War sent him back to Germany, and in the twenties he founded in Munich a celebrated art school, devoting himself for a quarter of a century mostly to teaching. When he arrived in America, in 1932, he was, if anything, an Expressionist. His painting became more and more abstract, and he was in the vanguard of those who took to flinging and dripping paint in what he called a "spiritual translation of inner concepts into form." He revived his school, teaching in New York in winter and in Provincetown in summer. Art critics said of him that he was an abstract expressionist, but no pigeonhole could contain him for long. His palette grew ever bolder and brighter, his brushwork more free—grand swipes of paint taking a blank canvas by storm. He worked fast and joyously, and he retained into his eighties, when much of his best work was accomplished, the zest of a youth on tiptoe.

Miguel Cervantes · 1 5 4 7 – 1 6 1 6

BY THE TIME the Spanish novelist and playwright Miguel Cervantes got around to writing his picaresque masterpiece, *Don Quixote,* he was in his late fifties. One reason for his tardiness may have been that he had devoted so much of his life to dangerous adventures. As a soldier, he fought and was wounded in the Battle of Lepanto, was later captured and enslaved by the viceroy of Algiers, and was finally ransomed with the help of his valorous mother. Returning to his native land, he married, wrote a number of plays, and pitched headlong into financial scrapes that caused him to be thrown into jail not once but several times. Few writers have led lives so vehement and so little rewarded except in terms of fame; on his deathbed he was still writing, and creditors were still knocking at the door.

As the hero of what is often defined as the first modern novel, Don Quixote, Knight of the Doleful Countenance, accompanied by his squire, Sancho Panza, wanders about the Spanish countryside seeking to perform those feats of idealistic knight-errantry that were the subject matter of the high-flown romances then popular in Spain. Cervantes was bent on destroying the pretensions of this species of literature by satirizing it. As so often happens with classic works, the satire has lost its sting over the centuries, but the superb comic inventiveness of the narrative endures. Cervantes knew that to be happy, old men must tilt their lances, even if their targets prove, by ill chance, only to be windmills.

Ellen Stewart ·

IN THE THIRTY-ODD YEARS Ellen Stewart has been presiding over the Cafe LaMaMa, on East Fourth Street in New York City, something like two thousand plays, musicals, and theater pieces of no conventionally identifiable sort have been put on there. The first Cafe LaMaMa was a shadowy basement space containing fifteen seats; today it consists of two big buildings furnished with four stages and a seating capacity of several hundred.

Stewart was enjoying a career as a dress designer when she undertook to finance the first Cafe LaMaMa out of her own pocket; she did so in order to help a member of her family, an aspiring playwright, get his works performed. In the early days, Ellen had to battle dozens of city rules and regulations in order to launch a cafe-cum-theater in the ramshackle quarters available to her; at least once she was thrown in jail for violating an ordinance her celebrated impatience had prompted her to ignore. She is equally short with play reviewers who, uneasy in the presence of the new and unexpected, fall back upon nonspecific adjectives like "experimental" and "provocative." Nor is she interested in the commercial success or failure of a play—only that it should be known to exist.

A thousand playwrights, from Samuel Beckett to Sam Shepherd, have been welcomed at Cafe LaMaMa; let the audiences make what they can of them. Ellen opens every performance by ringing a big old-fashioned brass school bell and speaking a few words of encouragement to the audience. For who knows what will happen next? Whatever it may be, LaMaMa, a true fostering mother, stands ready to usher it into the world.

O. Henry · 1862–1910

AN UNASSUMING LITTLE MAN named William Sydney Porter achieved fame in his middle years as a short-story writer, but took care to conceal his identity behind the pseudonym O. Henry. The bleak brevity of the pseudonym—not even so much as a first name but only the empty roundness of "O"—may have been prompted by something besides modesty: there was a dark chapter in his life, as strange and in many ways as unexpected as any of the events described in his stories, with their intricate plots and surprise endings.

Born in North Carolina, Porter set out as a young man to make his fortune in the West. In 1894, while employed as a bank teller in Austin, Texas, he was found to have "borrowed" money from the bank. He had done so partly to pay medical bills for his wife, who had come down with tuberculosis, and partly to finance the publication of a literary magazine he called *The Rolling Stone.*

Misconduct on behalf of a sick wife earned him sympathy; misconduct on behalf of a new literary magazine did not. In the ensuing scandal, Porter vanished. Three years later, having learned that his wife was dying, he returned to Austin, stood trial, was convicted of embezzlement, and spent three years in jail, where he began to write. Once out of jail, with his wife dead and a second marriage having failed, he took off for New York City, which in his stories he called "Baghdad on the Subway." For his thousands of enthralled readers, New York became a place charged with mystery and romance.

Porter died as quietly as he had lived. To a friend saying goodbye to him as the end neared, Porter gently quoted the chorus of a popular song of the day: "Don't turn out the light—I'm afraid to go home in the dark."

Larry Aldrich · BORN 1906

THE ALDRICH MUSEUM OF CONTEMPORARY ART, located in the historic old town of Ridgefield, Connecticut, is the creation of a slender, dapper, and witty man named Larry Aldrich, who in his youth amassed a fortune in the garment trade. Having started to collect art, he found that his interest lay in the encouragement of unknown artists, most of whom were in need of money. Today, at ninety, Aldrich continues to seek out the new in art, to support it financially, and to savor what he calls "happy surprises." Born of Russian Jewish immigrant parents, he grew up in a high-stooped brownstone in New York City and was expected to pursue a career in law. During a summer vacation when he was sixteen, he made so much money working in the garment district that he postponed further education in favor of purchasing a sporty red Oakland roadster and other symbols of worldly success. By twenty-one he was in charge of his own company. As a collector, Aldrich found himself running out of walls on which to hang his acquisitions. He thought of buying a house in Ridgefield to serve as a private art gallery, but his friend Alfred Barr, of the Museum of Modern Art, persuaded him to make it instead a museum open to the public. A favorite family "happy surprise," Aldrich speaking: "My father as a young man was required to serve in the Russian army. He was a crack shot, and when he won a competition in marksmanship the commanding officer of the regiment was so proud of him that he said he would grant him any request. Like all wellborn Russians of that day, the officer spoke immaculate English. My father, being eager to come to America, begged the officer to teach him English. The officer consented, and so it came about that my father arrived in this country as a penniless immigrant speaking English with an Oxford accent."

Laurence Sterne · 1 7 1 3 - 1 7 6 8

TO BE A CLERGYMAN in the Church of England in the eighteenth century wasn't necessarily to be a devout man of God—often enough, it consisted of being the poor relation of someone of wealth and position, upon whom one was obliged, in the course of seeking favors, to fawn as convincingly as possible. Failing rapid advancement, a man of the cloth would settle for a quiet, well-paying vicarage in an agreeable countryside, with the hope of attending jolly house parties, flirting with neighbors' wives, and enjoying occasional visits to the grand metropolis of London.

This was roughly the career of Laurence Sterne until, in his middle forties, he sat down to write what was to become over several years and in nine volumes one of the great comic novels of all time, *Tristram Shandy.* How in the world had this singular-looking little man, with his sharp nose and dreadful cough (much of his life was spent dying of tuberculosis), come to write such a work, which the London literary set instantly hailed as a masterpiece and which the public turned into an unprecedented best-seller? Idle to ask—he had astonished himself as well as the world.

In the first flush of Sterne's success, David Garrick praised him and Sir Joshua Reynolds painted his portrait; only the gruff and mighty Dr. Samuel Johnson demurred, asserting incorrectly of *Tristram Shandy,* "Nothing odd will do long." Equally odd and equally lasting is a book that Sterne, feverish social butterfly and indefatigable philanderer, wrote about his travels in France. He called it *A Sentimental Journey,* and it, too, became a best-seller. Said the happy author almost at the moment of death, "To write a book is for all the world like humming a song." And for him it was.

Grandma Moses · 1 8 6 0 – 1 9 6 1

ANNA MARY RICHARDSON was born in a small town in upstate New York. After a few years of "book-larnin'" acquired in a one-room schoolhouse characteristic of rural America in the post–Civil War period, she became what was known as a hired girl. (The word "servant" was frowned on in nineteenth-century America. Even in the houses of the rich, one employed "help" and not servants.) Anna Mary married a farmer named Moses and settled down in Eagle Bridge, New York, where she remained for the rest of her hundred-year-long life. She achieved a certain local fame for her skill in embroidery; at the age of seventy-six, arthritis forced her to abandon this art and she turned for the first time to painting.

Her subject matter consisted of those episodes of farm life that she had experienced firsthand or that had come down to her in stories told by family members gathered at night around the kitchen stove. She painted her canvases with the straightforward approach and honest emotion of a child, using primary colors and perspectives distorted according to her narrative needs. She was "discovered" in her eighties and made much of as a so-called primitive painter—a genre that happened to be gaining popularity at the time and that led to her being given exhibitions at the Museum of Modern Art, in New York City, and in other museums and galleries. If the world saw her as a classic late bloomer and dared to patronize her with the nickname "Grandma," the world was welcome to its big-city ways; Anna Mary Richardson Moses went on being who she was and painting as she pleased—more than 600 canvases in all—and the purity of her handiwork never faltered into self-consciousness.

Samuel Hayakawa · 1906–1992

FEW STATESMEN COME LATE TO FAME in a democracy, since the difficult art of being elected to office usually requires practice in running for office, even for so lowly a post as dogcatcher. Samuel Hayakawa was a notable exception; he was elected a United States senator from California at the age of seventy, having little or no previous political experience. Born in Canada, he earned graduate degrees in English at McGill University and at the University of Wisconsin, where, acquiring American citizenship, he began work as a teacher. He ended his academic career as president of San Francisco State College. It was a time when many scholars were devoting themselves to the study of the nature of speech and language—a once simple-seeming attribute of humankind that was beginning to be regarded as highly complex and mysterious. Hayakawa served as editor of the magazine *ETC*, which devoted itself to semantics, most easily defined as "the science of the meaning of words." What, Hayakawa would ask, is the role of verbal communication in human affairs, especially at a moment when the hundreds of languages spoken throughout the world estrange nations that have the most to gain by drawing together? Or what of the fact that even in one's own language a given word may induce a radically different response in every individual that hears it? Hayakawa and contemporaries like Count Alfred Korzybski and Benjamin Lee Whorf sought some practical means of making it clear that words are not things, existing "out there" in space, with immutable denotations and connotations, but are instead temporary approximations of our ideas *about* things. Their efforts gained a certain measure of popularity after the Second World War, but had no lasting effect: we go on misunderstanding one another with undiminished relish and despair.

Eugene Atget · 1857-1927

PHOTOGRAPHY FROM ITS BIRTH was closely allied with architecture, and not least because photographs in their early days required long time exposures, and streets and buildings had the advantage over human beings of being by their nature immobile—in effect, it was easy to have them sit for their portraits. In history, unquestionably the most gifted taker of such portraits is a gentle failed actor and failed painter named Eugene Atget, who, fearing failure in any other occupation, spent much of the latter part of an impoverished life documenting the ancient districts of Paris and its environs—districts that, thanks to Baron Haussmann's plans for the demolition and reconstruction of Paris, were then rapidly vanishing.

Using an old-fashioned bellows camera on a wooden tripod, Atget trudged about Paris year after year, accumulating more than ten thousand photographs of buildings, bridges, alleyways, doorways, and the like. He sold these photographs for a few francs apiece to stage designers, artists, and decorators in search of picturesque subject matter and to museums and historians needing accurate information about the city's obliterated past. Late in life, Atget's handiwork came to the attention of a neighbor, the American artist and experimental photographer Man Ray, who surprisingly hailed Atget as a surrealist. Ray's student Berenice Abbott, later to become well known as a documentary photographer, purchased Atget's prints and negatives after his death and helped to spread the reputation of his having been, in her words, "a Balzac of the camera." The Abbott Collection, which includes hundreds of Atgets, is at the Museum of Modern Art, in New York City.

Mother Teresa · 1 9 1 0 - 1 9 9 7

AGNES BOJAXHIU, known throughout the world as Mother Teresa, was born in 1910 in the city of Skopje, in what was then Albania. Many people believe her to have been a saint, though not of a conventional sort. She has been described as having a "wrinkled brown peasant face, lumpy nose, long teeth, and black glittery eyes . . . tough and alert, no saintly Madonna." From her earliest years she was determined to devote her life to the poor and ill, and to that end, while still in her teens, she left home to join the Sisters of Loretto, a community of Irish nuns with a mission house in the Archdiocese of Calcutta. She took her first vows as a nun at eighteen and her final vows some nine years later. It wasn't until she was forty that she was able to launch her Missionaries of Charity as an official religious community in Calcutta; fifteen years later, the Vatican recognized it as a pontifical congregation, worthy of being placed under its immediate supervision. By then, Sister Teresa's Home for the Dying Destitute, in Calcutta, had become well known. Her organization had established mission houses in cities in every corner of the globe, with hundreds of nuns under Mother Teresa's guidance providing food, shelter, schooling, and clinical care in every corner of the globe.

It was characteristic of Mother Teresa's peasant directness that when Pope Paul VI visited her in India, in 1964, and being much impressed by her labors presented her with his big white Lincoln Continental limousine, she saw to it that the limousine was instantly auctioned off and turned into cash for the poor. In her seventies and eighties, she traveled unflaggingly from miserable slum to slum in country after country, championing a cause she defined in eight heart-breaking words: "Concern for those who are unwanted and unloved."

Ian Fleming · 1 9 0 8 – 1 9 6 4

IN A LIFE AS SHORT AS Ian Fleming's, to bloom late amounts to a manner of speaking. If this gifted writer had lived to what has become in our time the commonplace of a ripe old age of eighty-five or ninety, it might have been said that he bloomed comparatively early, having produced the first of his thrillers about the irresistible James Bond when he was forty-five. By then, he had succeeded in a number of careers—as a journalist, banker, and stockbroker. In World War II he served as a member of His Majesty's Naval Intelligence Division, where he acquired his inside knowledge of the intricacies of spying.

After the war, he became the foreign manager of a group of British newspapers, resigning in 1959 to devote himself entirely to writing. At his winter home in Jamaica he turned out, at the astonishing rate of one a year, a series of novels recounting the adventures of Secret Agent 007, a character who, embodied in the movies by the puissant and urbane Sean Connery, soon became world famous and made his creator—to say nothing of Connery—deservedly famous as well.

Ian Fleming was the younger brother of the well-known writer and explorer Peter Fleming and the husband of a granddaughter of the eleventh Earl of Wemyss, which is to say that he knew his way about in a pukka-sahib milieu unfamiliar to most thriller-writers and thriller-readers. Bond's social and sexual prowess fill us with a bearable envy; we are quick to identify ourselves with him, whether at a ball or in a bedroom or when, facing death at the hands of evil adversaries, he proceeds unflappably to outwit them. Like any well-brought-up Brit, Fleming pretended to be something of an amateur as a writer, though in fact Secret Agent 007 is likely to prove as immortal as Sherlock Holmes.

Odilon Redon · 1 8 4 0 – 1 9 1 6

THE NOTION OF THE ARTIST as somebody who by dint of hard work makes his way up out of poverty to gain fame and fortune is so fixed in our imaginations that we tend to doubt whether any wealthy youth could possibly attain the same depth of accomplishment, much less deserve to do so. Something in our half-buried puritanical culture prefers the first notion to the second, though not a shred of evidence exists to substantiate it. A rich young person begins with a mighty advantage over a poor one, and history teaches us that this advantage is often fully utilized.

A case in point is the French artist Odilon Redon, whose wealth may be said to have proved a handicap to him only to the extent that he could afford to take his time, and so he took it. His father, a citizen of Bordeaux, was a highly successful cotton merchant in the Mississippi Delta; his mother, also of French origin, was born in New Orleans. (The Degas family had similar American cotton connections.) Redon was born and raised in Bordeaux, took his first drawing lessons at fifteen, studied architecture in his twenties, and drifted into the study of painting at the École des Beaux Arts, in Paris. After serving in the Franco-Prussian War and paying several extended visits to Holland and Belgium, where he studied the Old Masters, he returned to Paris and took up, under the tutelage of Fantin-Latour, the then novel medium of lithography. He achieved renown in his forties as the creator of "decadent" fantasies of a perverse and never-quite-to-be-revealed sexual nature and as an illustrator of books by Flaubert and Baudelaire. At fifty he produced his first pastels and oils and at sixty he began the gorgeous flower studies that have made him immortal. In the famous Armory Show of 1913, held in New York City, Redon had more paintings on exhibition than any other artist.

Jonathan Swift · 1 6 6 7 - 1 7 4 5

THAT IRASCIBLE CLERIC Jonathan Swift was fifty-nine when he gained fame as the author of *Gulliver's Travels.* Being one of those people who accumulate grievances as naturally as other people breathe, he felt strongly that popular recognition of his talents was long overdue. In expurgated form, his account of the adventures of Lemuel Gulliver has become an enduring children's classic, but Swift had intended it to be no such thing—he wrote it as a virulent satire on human folly in general and, in particular, on the social and political follies he observed firsthand during his extended stays in England.

Though Swift was born and educated in Ireland—contemporary scholars believe him to have been the bastard son of his benefactor, Sir William Temple—and as a clergyman earned his living there, he much preferred residing in London, where he wrote political tracts and won the friendship of Pope, Steele, and other prominent literary figures. He was appointed Dean of St. Patrick's Cathedral, in Dublin, in 1713. In that high office, he was a member of the local Anglo-Irish ruling class, but to the consternation of colleagues he took the side of the Catholic Irish in their political struggle to free themselves from British rule. In one of the bitterest satires ever written, entitled *A Modest Proposal*, he advocated the breeding of Irish babies, who to reduce Ireland's poverty would be sold at a good price to the rich and be eaten by them.

Swift divided his attentions between two women, both of whom he vexed and neither of whom he married. His mentally clouded old age would today almost certainly identify him as a victim of Alzheimer's disease. He composed the epitaph for the tomb in which he lies buried in St. Patrick's; it says of him that in death savage indignation can no longer lacerate his heart.

Jacques-Henri Lartigue ·

ONE OF THE MOST AGREEABLE FORMS of blooming late is to have bloomed early without the knowledge of the world beyond one's doorstep and then, on being discovered in old age, to find the world crowding that doorstep and singing one's praises. This was the happy fate of Jacques-Henri Lartigue, who at seven was given by his father, himself an amateur photographer, a large box camera on a wooden tripod.

Master Lartigue started taking photographs of members of his wealthy family and of family friends as they amused themselves in the suburbs of Paris during the years of La Belle Epoque. Like Alice Austen in America at approximately the same time, he was eager to catch people off guard and in a carefree mood, whether cycling or flying kites or attending balloon and automobile races or simply, with innocent abandon, floating in a pool or leaping down a flight of garden steps.

Young as he was, Lartigue had an eye and he acquired a high degree of technical skill in stopping action without blurring and in the manipulation of available light. By the time the First World War broke out, Lartigue had lost interest in still photography. He had decided to become a painter and soon gained a considerable reputation in that field. The photographs taken in boyhood were published by *Life* in 1963, and the following year an exhibition of them was held at the Museum of Modern Art, in New York City. Lartigue was saluted by Richard Avedon and other young lions. The handsome and charming old man enjoyed being made much of for work that by then might have been created by a total stranger and therefore required of him no formal pretext of modesty. *"Bien sûr,* how delightful they were, those family souvenirs!" he would exclaim. "But then how delightful the times were as well, not to be seen anymore."

Ruth Gordon • 1 8 9 6 - 1 9 8 5

HENRY JAMES SAID THAT we are all young to life, the passage of years being what he called a slow, reluctant march into enemy country—"the country of the general lost freshness." It was James's theory that if we contrived not to lose that freshness, we would, in effect, never grow old, and there are people who demonstrate the truth of this dictum by remaining as open to change at seventy as they were at twenty, spunkily confronting the world and finding in it up to the last moment a fruitful place in which to function.

The actress Ruth Gordon was such a person. Born in Worcester, Massachusetts, she set her sights early on becoming an actress. Studying at the American Academy of Dramatic Arts, in New York City, she made her stage debut in a revival of *Peter Pan* that starred Maude Adams, the American creator of the role. Gordon herself starred in successful Broadway plays like *Saturday's Children, Serena Blandish, Ethan Frome,* and *A Doll's House.* She wrote two plays— *Over 21* and *Years Ago*—and an autobiography called *Myself Among Others.*

She was married for many years to the writer Garson Kanin, and they became famous as a couple, collaborating on literary work and having their topical witticisms quoted in the press. The movie *Harold and Maude,* in which Gordon plays a harum-scarum old lady with whom a teenage boy falls in love, was an unexpected hit and gave a new turn to her career. Gordon's voice had a sharp New England rasp, which added to the humor of her delivery. Having known everyone and done everything, jubilantly she went on talking and talking and there were few who wished to interrupt her.

Charles Ives · 1874–1954

THE AMERICAN COMPOSER Charles Ives was every bit as eccentric in character as he was in his music and remained resolutely at odds with the dominant culture of his day, gaining fame only in old age and still greater fame after his death. Much of his music—reckless in its mingling of ragtime, jazz, hymns, and experimental dissonances—he never heard played in public. When he received a Pulitzer Prize in 1947 for his Third Symphony (which he had written forty-three years earlier), he made haste to give the prize money to a fellow composer, who needed it more than he did. For Ives, unlike most composers known to history, was an astute businessman and had early made a substantial fortune selling life insurance.

Born in Danbury, Connecticut, Ives was raised by a father who, as a local bandmaster and church organist, manifested a radically adventurous musical spirit, trying (as he used to say of himself) to locate and duplicate instrumentally "the sounds that fall between the cracks." On graduating from Yale, Ives moved to New York, where, selling insurance by day and composing by night, he introduced into his compositions the rattle of trolley cars and other urban noises. The titles he affixed to his pieces—"Some Southpaw Pitches," "General William Booth Enters into Heaven"—were as unexpected as the pieces themselves.

Ives married Harmony Twitchell, daughter of Mark Twain's close friend and hiking companion the Reverend Joseph Twitchell. It was thought that the bride's name was highly appropriate; in fact, harmony in the usual sense was the last thing Ives wished to pursue. Living in a brownstone directly across the street from one of New York City's most admired schools of music, the white-bearded old man would stand in a front-parlor window and shake his fist at students approaching the school, urging them silently not to enter.

Richard Robert Wright · 1853–1947

RICHARD ROBERT WRIGHT was born into slavery on a cotton plantation near Dalton, Georgia, and died as one of the most prominent bankers in Philadelphia—a career he adopted in his late sixties, in order to demonstrate to ambitious young black people that banking was just as useful a path to success as medicine or the law. As a child, one of Wright's tasks was to keep flies off the dining room table in his master's house, swinging a big punkah back and forth above the food. He was engaged in that activity when he heard the Master discussing the latest news— the freeing of the slaves. That was in 1865. The Master offered to keep Wright's family on as paid help, but the family refused the offer. Many years later, when Wright had begun to make a name for himself, the Master wrote him a letter, taking credit for having given him his start in the world. "Him that once caught me reading out of a speller," Wright would say, "and threw the speller into the stove and gave me a thrashing. Some start he gave me!"

Wright's mother walked him and his sister to Atlanta and enrolled them in a newly founded school there, which later became Atlanta University. After graduation, Wright taught school, helped organize the state's first public high school for blacks, and founded the Georgia State Industrial College, which he headed until 1921. By then, he was a prominent figure in the Republican Party. Over the years he enjoyed an acquaintance with every president from Rutherford B. Hayes to Harry S. Truman. He hit on Philadelphia as the ideal place to start his bank, which he called the Citizens and Southern Bank & Trust Company, after a bank back home in Georgia that had once refused to do business with one of his daughters.

Piet Mondrian · 1 8 7 2 - 1 9 4 4

THE DUTCH ARTIST PIET MONDRIAN was slow to devise a method of putting paint on canvas that seemed to him appropriate to his intellectual convictions. He was slower still to gain favorable reception for the results he secured by this method, but fame was the least of his concerns. For people who are happy in what they do, there is neither early nor late in respect to when they bloom; there is only the pleasure of the now.

As a student in Amsterdam, Mondrian worked his way conscientiously through painting in the approved academic fashion and later, in Paris, through the pioneering experiments of the cubists as well. Back in the Netherlands, he helped to found the De Stijl movement and sought to render the tenets of Theosophy graphically manifest. Before the Second World War, Mondrian moved to New York City, whose skyscrapers and jazz music delighted him. The method of painting he had arrived at by then consisted of a seemingly arbitrary deployment of horizontal and vertical lines that form large and small rectangular boxes of sunny, primary colors—abstract constructions that strike the viewer as being implacable in the limits the artist has imposed on them and yet uncannily free and merry-hearted. We sense that the artist has made himself all the more present by dint of his absence, having taken care to omit all the usual signposts of personality. But of course the artist is intensely there; he is to be detected in every ingeniously calculated square inch of his canvases. Mondrian's most famous painting, owned by the Museum of Modern Art, is *Broadway Boogie-Woogie.* In it we observe the old Netherlandish bachelor contentedly dancing to a New World beat.

Isabelle Stevenson • BORN 1915

ISABELLE STEVENSON is the head of the American Theatre Wing, the oldest and by common consent one of the most useful service organizations in the chaotic world of Broadway. Its best-known activity is the annual bestowal of the Tony Awards, named after Antoinette Perry, a founder of the Wing. Broadway has been familiar to Stevenson ever since she made her debut as a dancer in Earl Carroll's *Vanities*, in the 1930s. Subsequently she realized every performer's dream by playing the Palace as a member of a vaudeville team called Nice, Florio, and Lubow (Lubow was her maiden name). Dressed in evening clothes, the trio did pratfalls and comedy and toured the country, sometimes playing on the same bill as Bob Hope. They became sufficiently celebrated to appear at the Palladium Theatre, in London, and to give a command performance for King George VI. In Paris, reviewing their performance at the Olympia Theatre, the newspaper *Figaro* described Lubow as "a blond Josephine Baker." In Hollywood, she took a screen test that made her look, so she humorously asserts today, "like a bad copy of Marlene Dietrich or a lesser Garbo."

Be that as it may, she gave up her theatrical career on marrying a New York businessman named John Stevenson and beginning a family. She joined the board of directors of the Wing in 1960 and became its president in 1965, starting a new and unlooked-for career as an executive at the age of fifty. 1996 marks the fiftieth anniversary of the American Theatre Wing, and Stevenson plans to make the most of this opportunity to acquaint the world with the many activities that, Tony Awards aside, the Wing regularly sponsors. Not by so much as a flicker of an eye does Stevenson indicate that one reason for the Wing's continued success is that she is, like the theater itself, an irresistible force.

John Houseman · 1 9 0 2 - 1 9 8 8

WHETHER BLOOMING EARLY OR LATE, few people have enjoyed a career as varied, starting from the cradle, as that of John Houseman. He was born Jacques Haussmann, in Bucharest, to an English mother and an Alsatian father, was dispatched to Argentina at the age of twenty-one to help further his father's grain business, moved to the United States for the same purpose, and began, under his newly Americanized name, to write and direct plays. In 1934 he scored a triumph with his direction on Broadway of the Gertrude Stein-Virgil Thomson opera, *Four Saints in Three Acts.* A year later, he formed a partnership with the twenty-year-old Orson Welles, directing and producing many plays under the banner of the Mercury Theater.

After a never-to-be-resolved quarrel with Welles, Houseman worked in Hollywood as a producer and, in the Second World War, served as chief of the overseas radio division of the Office of War Information. When the war was over, Houseman commuted between Hollywood and New York, producing movies on one coast and directing plays and TV specials on the other. In 1967 he became head of the drama division at the Juilliard School of Music and founded a repertory troupe called The Acting Company. In his seventies, he started a highly successful acting career, winning an Oscar for his performance as a crusty old Harvard professor of law in *The Paper Chase.* Later, Houseman was amused to earn large sums as a spokesman in TV commercials for a Wall Street brokerage house. Meanwhile, he became the best-selling author of three volumes of autobiography. For many years, he maintained a country house a few miles north of New York City, where, so he said with mock dismay, he would listen to his hundred-year-old mother telling him the same stories that she had told to little Jacques in Bucharest some eighty years before.

Louis Jacques Mandé Daguerre · 1 7 8 7 - 1 8 5 1

LOUIS JACQUES MANDÉ DAGUERRE was in his early fifties when he announced to
the French Academy, in Paris, and from that lofty platform to the world at large
the invention of the method of photography that bears his name. He had been a
long time arriving at the means of chemically fixing a likeness in permanent form,
and having succeeded in doing so he was content to offer the invention to the
French government and to accept in return a pension and a much-prized member-
ship in the Legion of Honor. He then retired to a village in the French countryside
and showed little interest in further advances in his invention. This valedictory
stepping aside may have been a wiser decision than he knew, for it turned out that
his method of producing images on metal proved to be a dead end; film and paper
were soon to win the day.

Daguerre was a slow mover as well as a late bloomer. After contemplating a
career in architecture, he had turned in his late teens to what struck him as an
easier and more lucrative way of earning a living, namely, scene painting. He became a student of Degotti, who was in charge of preparing sets at the Paris Opera,
and spent a couple of decades doggedly painting canvas flats backstage. In 1822 he
and a colleague, Charles Bouton, developed the diorama, a method of displaying
pictures that creates animated visual effects. Daguerre manufactured dioramas for
the next seventeen years, until the drudgery of having to reproduce by hand the
same scenes over and over exhausted his patience and he sought a shortcut—some
means of preserving images out of the past for use in the future. In collaboration
with a fellow Parisian, J. N. Niepce, he contrived to discover that shortcut, demon-
strating that boredom as well as necessity can be the mother of invention.

Isaac Hirschfeld · 1 8 6 7 - 1 9 5 9

THE CARICATURIST AL HIRSCHFELD, now entering his ninety-fourth year, is the opposite of a late bloomer; at seventeen he secured a job drawing advertisements for a movie company and was soon to be seen scorching about New York City in a snappy Stutz Bearcat roadster and frequenting fashionable speakeasies—the epitome in the Jazz Age of someone who had hit the big time. It is Hirschfeld's father, Isaac Hirschfeld, who was a late bloomer, and a late bloomer of a peculiar kind—one who never held a regular job until he was seventy-five. While his wife supported him and their family by working as a saleslady at Wertheimer's Department Store, Isaac was to be found in a nearby sandlot, playing catch with his sons and their companions. It seems everyone, not least his wife and children, so enjoyed his company that it would never have crossed their minds to protest his indolence. In old age, Isaac bestirred himself to fight political battles in behalf of the economic benefits due his contemporaries—those hardworking old folk who up to then he had taken care to keep a prudent distance from. According to lexicographers, Isaac invented and popularized the term "senior citizen."

In his nineties, getting ready to die, Isaac summoned his family to the hospital. He appeared to be trying to make some sort of profound deathbed statement, and the family hovered over his bed in order not to miss a single word. At last he spoke: "The nurses around here," he said, "are big enough to be playing professional football."

Margot Gayle · BORN 1908

A HEROIC FIGURE IN THE STRUGGLE to preserve the architectural heritage of New York City, Margot Gayle came north from her native state of Georgia in the 1920s bent on taking a useful part in the cultural life of the city. Over the years, she came to see how little native New Yorkers appeared to mourn the continuous destruction of old buildings that embodied the city's past. To knock the city down and build it up again every twenty or thirty years was progress—the never-look-back American way, which had been followed locally ever since a Dutch trading post was established on the tip of Manhattan island in the early seventeenth century.

As a private citizen, middle-aged and without private means, Margot Gayle set about changing that perverse tradition. When the Jefferson Market Courthouse, a Victorian edifice in the heart of Greenwich Village, was threatened with demolition in 1959, she rallied the neighborhood in its defense and helped to give it a new purpose as a branch of the New York Public Library. From that victory emerged the Victorian Society in America, founded in Gayle's kitchen. A few years later, and almost singlehandedly, she saved the district now known as SoHo—the largest remaining accumulation of nineteenth-century cast-iron buildings in existence. From that second victory emerged an organization called the Friends of Cast-Iron, which flourishes to this day. Next came the creation of an official city agency, the Landmarks Preservation Commission, which presides over many historic districts and individual buildings in all five boroughs of the city. At eighty-six, Gayle continues to be a leading figure in the preservation movement, and at any public meeting held in City Hall to discuss that topic the indomitable Gayle is sure to be found in the front row, making her voice—still Georgian in accent—gently but distinctly heard.

Roger Horchow • BORN 1928

GAINING SUCCESS in a certain field of endeavor can tempt a person into seeking to achieve similar success in a second field—often, and unwisely, one totally unlike the first. Many businessmen over the years have assumed that because they have prospered by manufacturing steel beams or women's dresses they will prosper as producers on Broadway—a notion having little or no basis in theatrical history. The most remarkable exception to the usual rule of failure in all such attempts is Roger Horchow, a Texas businessman who from childhood had been devoted to the music of George Gershwin and had cherished the hope of someday undertaking a revival of the Gershwin musical *Girl Crazy.*

In his sixties, Horchow sold his catalogue business for an extremely large sum. Having made generous gifts to various good causes, he gathered his family together and asked them to put to a vote the question of whether he should gamble nine or ten million dollars on something that he had never done before and that was known to be one of the riskiest enterprises on earth, even for professional insiders. Put on a Broadway musical? The family said, in effect, "Go for it, Pop!" and he did.

The result was *Crazy for You,* drawn partly from *Girl Crazy* and partly from other material the Gershwin heirs were eager to have produced. Horchow presided over every last detail of the production, which opened in February 1992 to rave reviews and ran on Broadway for several years. Road companies of the show are currently playing in England, France, Japan, Australia, and other distant countries, and the likelihood is that it will be playing somewhere on earth ten or twenty years from now. Meanwhile, Horchow is risking failure by succumbing to still another outlandish temptation: he is writing a book about his success as a Broadway producer.

Sarah Tomerlin Lee · BORN 19??

IT OFTEN HAPPENS THAT through the passage of time the victim of a tragic event gains from the consequences of it an increased strength of purpose, a multiplied capability vis-a-vis the world. Sarah Tomerlin Lee has been one of the leading interior designers of hotels and other public and semipublic buildings in the United States over the past quarter-century. She undertook this career only after the sudden death from a heart attack of her husband, Tom Lee, founder of an interior design firm that bore his name and was long prominent in the field. Up to that time, Sarah Lee had enjoyed a career complementary to but distinct from her husband's. Born in Tennessee, she graduated from Randolph Macon College in 1932, came north to New York City, and was hired as an advertising copywriter at Bonwit Teller department store. In rapid stages, she became first a vice president of Lord & Taylor department store and then editor in chief of *House Beautiful.* In her years as head of Tom Lee, Inc., she has supervised the design, or redesign, of over forty major hotels, including the old Willard, in Washington, D.C., and the new Palace and Parker-Meridien, in New York City. She has also helped to refurbish interior spaces in such historically significant public buildings as the New York City Hall, which dates back to 1803. Lee was a founding member of the New York Landmarks Conservancy, which has been instrumental in saving, nearly always against high odds, dozens of examples of early New York City architecture. In her mid-eighties, Sarah Tomerlin Lee—invariably wearing a broad-brimmed hat and gloves, the epitome of old-fashioned elegance of dress and deportment—remains active in the practice of her profession as head of the interior design division of the architectural firm of Beyer, Blinder, Belle.

Ferdinand von Zeppelin ·

HOW CAN IT HELP BUT BE a matter of pride when, for whatever reason, one's name advances from uppercase to lowercase, from the particular to the universal? And all the more so if one has happened to play an otherwise obscure role in the history of one's time. This was the agreeable fate of Count Ferdinand von Zeppelin, whose name has become the generic term for a certain kind of lighter-than-air machine, invented late in his life and successfully flown years before the Wright Brothers found themselves swooping over the dunes at Kitty Hawk. Born in the kingdom of Württemberg, the young Count, a fearless professional soldier, took off for America and fought on the Union side in the Civil War. Meeting Lincoln, he said to him, "The Zeppelins have been counts for centuries." Lincoln replied, "That will not be in your way if you behave well as a soldier."

The Count fought gallantly under General Hooker's command, but it was love of battle that dominated him, not the Union cause; he kept in his pocket a letter of introduction to General Lee. Zeppelin made his first balloon ascension during his stay in America, and it occurred to him then that the next step would be an airborne vehicle capable of being propelled and steered—in short, a dirigible. Many years later, living in retirement in Württemberg, he set to work designing one. Hydrogen-filled, with rudders for steering and gasoline engines to propel them, the first four zeppelins the Count built suffered a variety of unlucky accidents; the fifth proved successful. Long after his death, high-speed heavier-than-air aircraft triumphed over lighter-than-air; dirigibles came to be used mostly to carry advertising on their round bellies and to help TV cameras cover sporting events from the air. No matter! The Count had had his day.

Betty Furness •

IN THE CONVENTIONAL SENSE, Betty Furness was by no means a late bloomer—born and brought up on Park Avenue, in New York City, she started blooming professionally as a model and movie actress in her teens. What is worthy of note is that she bloomed late as well as early, with undiminished zest, in a variety of careers.

Invited to Hollywood, she starred in some thirty B movies, few of them memorable. She was pretty and wholesome-looking and fatally lacked allure. In her day, the big studios were in constant fear lest the so-called masculinity of some of their major male stars, indispensable at the box office, might be rendered suspect in published gossip about their private lives. Furness good-naturedly served as the supposed favorite "date" of Cary Grant, when Grant was enjoying an affair with the New York photographer Jerry Zerbe. Furness and Grant would be seen having dinner at Dave Chasen's popular restaurant and Furness would be back in her apartment by ten.

In 1949 she became one of the highest paid performers on TV, peddling with vivacious conviction the quality of Westinghouse refrigerators. Almost twenty years later, she switched from attracting customers to protecting them. President Johnson appointed her his special assistant for consumer affairs, and a few years later, she became commissioner of the Department of Consumer Affairs in New York City. People trusted her because she seemed in her well-bred way incapable of stooping to deceive them. Writing for magazines and newspapers and making a weekly appearance on the TV show *Today*, she became a classic celebrity of and for our time—one of those persons famous for being well known. It is only a B role, but she played it well.

Cliff May · 1 9 0 8 – 1 9 8 9

THERE ARE PEOPLE WHO, blooming early in respect to their talent, bloom late in reputation. One thinks of Cliff May, the premier practitioner of what has come to be known as the California ranch house style of architecture. For well over fifty years, ranch houses designed by May were eagerly sought after and could be found in places as remote from California as Venezuela, Switzerland, the Caribbean, and even Ireland, facing the rainy, windswept North Atlantic. His houses were admired by no less a person than Frank Lloyd Wright, whose usual principle was to sneer at the handiwork of any architect except himself. Wright's prairie houses and May's ranch houses have much in common: a simple, natural use of stone and wood, immense gabled roofs with broad overhangs, a profile running parallel to the earth and seeming to grow out of it. Like Wright, May was a maverick, but unlike Wright he was a modest one. He had never gone to architectural school and had not been licensed to practice architecture; during most of his long career he was permitted to be called merely a designer. "It took architects a long time to let me into the club," he said once. "The same with architectural critics and historians. They're starting to pay attention to me now, in my old age. No hard feelings on my part! I was always having too much fun to hang around waiting for some professor to praise me." Off Sunset Boulevard, in Los Angeles, May bought a tract of land in the 1930s that embraced an entire canyon. He filled the canyon with cozy houses built to his design and sold them with the understanding that they would be occupied only by families with children and horses. To this day a visitor drives up the narrow, winding road of the canyon past a series of miniature ranches teeming with children, horses, and dogs: May country and so happy country.

Edith Wharton · 1862-1937

EDITH WHARTON WAS BORN Edith Newbold Jones, at a time when the Newbolds and the Joneses were considered the cream of New York City society and the Vanderbilts mere pushy outsiders. Strictly brought up within the limits thought appropriate to young women in those days, Miss Jones was fobbed off in marriage to Edward Wharton, a proper Boston banker. What little the bride knew about sex appears to have struck her as unpleasant, and her hapless bridegroom did little to alter that opinion. Indeed, it wasn't until she was in her forties and long divorced from Teddie that an American newspaperman living in London was able to provide her, in an unexpected tryst in an unfashionable hotel bedroom, with what was then known as an "awakening."

Wharton was almost equally late in coming into her vocation as a novelist. She had always read voraciously and in her apprentice years modeled herself on Henry James, who became her friend. They shared as subject matter the social world into which they had been born, whose customs they depicted and whose lack of moral vision they deplored.

Wharton remained unmarried and maintained a great house, the Mount, in Lenox, Massachusetts, and a couple of residences in the French countryside. When James visited her at the Mount, they rejoiced in going automobiling together. In goggles and linen dusters, they sat in the back of a big open car and urged the chauffeur to go faster and faster along the narrow, winding roads of the Berkshire hills: middle-aged children contentedly at play.

Jean Dubuffet · 1901–1985

ONE IS ALWAYS TEMPTED to detect a likeness between a work of art and its maker, and in the case of the French artist Jean Dubuffet the temptation becomes irresistible. He was a short, bald, heavy-featured man, who looked as if he had lumbered up out of the Stone Age in none too good a temper, and his paintings nearly always conveyed a similarly harsh impression—accumulations of pigment mixed with sand, putty, ashes, and other found materials. His strangulated amoeboid sculptures were made of concrete painted black and white, as if to assert the degree of their separation from the variegated hues of nature.

Dubuffet's life was a continuous struggle against the bourgeois conventions that he deplored and yet kept having to retreat to. His father was a prosperous wine and liquor merchant in Le Havre, and in after years, accounting for his having quit Le Havre in his late teens to make his way as an artist in Paris, he said bluntly, "I hated my family, with its constant talk of money."

To his dismay, he was obliged on several occasions to return to selling wine because his experiments in art failed to provide him with even the bleakest of livings. It was in his forties that Dubuffet began to be taken seriously by the critics, who accepted his dictum that what he called *art brut*, or raw art—an art also to be found in the creative efforts of children, criminals, and madmen—had something of value to offer the world. Becoming a fashionable artist, he went on railing with his usual perverse gusto against fashion. Rich, he salved his conscience by wearing blue jeans and nursing his lifelong gift for wrath.

Gertrude Jekyll · 1843–1932

REVOLUTIONS TAKE PLACE in gardening as well as in governments. A hard-headed spinster named Gertrude Jekyll was a leader in the overturning of the conventional Victorian garden, with its beds of flowers set out in geometric shapes and the flowers themselves unnaturally separated according to color and species.

Born to wealth and social position, Jekyll received almost no formal education—well-bred daughters of that period were thought to be at risk of overheating their brains if they were obliged to think. It was enough that young Gertrude, having artistic talent, should busy herself with painting watercolors, working in silver, and doing embroidery.

Jekyll's eyesight began to fail her in her late thirties, forcing her to give up embroidery and other fine handiwork and turn to gardening. With her own garden serving as a testing ground, she launched an attack upon the laborious artificiality of the gardens then in fashion. The great event of her life was encountering, in middle age, the twenty-year-old Edwin Lutyens—a dazzling young architect, who was to design many of the handsomest country houses ever built in the British Isles. Jekyll undertook to lay out the gardens that accompanied Lutyens's houses, and she proved as skillful as he was at getting her way with hesitant clients. Her purpose was always to make a strong plan and then have it appear to be entirely natural, with an abundance of native plants and herbs, their colors blending together and their fragrance an element more important than mere large, showy blooms. With Lutyens starting so early and Jekyll starting so late, they became an indissoluble team, whose fame will last as long as her roses climb his walls.

Georges Eugene Haussmann · 1809-1891

IT IS IN THE NATURE OF CITIES TO CHANGE, often enough for the better, but in Paris it is especially the case that every change is mourned by those who recall the city as it existed in their youth. But that city, too, had once been new and unwelcome. Henry James in age vehemently regretted that so much of *his* Paris, a quasi-medieval Paris of crooked streets and dark, half-timbered houses crouching behind ancient fortified walls, had been destroyed by the ruthless urban planning of Baron Georges Eugene Haussmann. The population of Paris had increased to a point where much of its housing had deteriorated into slums and its meager infrastructure—water supply, sewage removal, and the like—was continuously breaking down. Haussmann demolished the old city walls and created handsome boulevards in their stead; he built more than three hundred miles of sewers, which became a favorite tourist attraction (and remain so to this day); and he planted a hundred thousand trees along some four hundred miles of new pavement. Haussmann carried out these radical improvements at the bidding of Emperor Napoleon III, a vulgar monarch whose interest in beautifying Paris was largely political: the straight boulevards could be readily defended against rioting revolutionaries, and the number of laborers required to knock down the scruffy old Paris and build a shining new one in its place served as a means of minimizing unemployment. The financial cost of what came to be dubbed "Haussmannomania" was very high. After spending the equivalent in today's money of two or three billion dollars, Haussmann was forced into retirement, to his bitter disappointment. He had spent his life preparing for the task and had only begun implementing it in his fifties and sixties. Like many another dismissed public servant throughout history, he took revenge by writing his memoirs.

Anne Meara · BORN 1929

ACTORS WHO HAVE ENJOYED SUCCESS speaking lines written by others are likely at a certain point in their careers to convince themselves that they, too, are capable of becoming playwrights. Impatiently—perhaps impertinently—they pose a question: as living persons on a stage, are they not better judges of what pleases an audience than an individual working alone in a hushed study somewhere far from the hurly-burly of the world of theater? Their question has a plausible ring to it, and history provides examples, from Shakespeare to Noel Coward, of actors turned playwrights whose literary mastery is sufficiently obvious.

A recent newly born actor-playwright is Anne Meara, author of the Off Broadway comedy *After-Play,* in which she also performs a major role. Meara studied acting with Alfred Linden and Uta Hagen, and played with Zero Mostel in *Ulysses in Nighttown,* Mostel's adaptation of a portion of Joyce's prodigious novel. She created the role of Bunny in John Guare's *The House of Blue Leaves* and acted the bawdy Nurse in Joseph Papp's production of *Romeo and Juliet.* She and her husband, Jerry Stiller, appeared as a comedy team on Ed Sullivan's TV show more than thirty-five times. On Broadway she won a Tony nomination for her performance in Eugene O'Neill's *Anna Christie.* Writing her first play in her middle sixties, she is content to be identified as a late bloomer, one who possesses a merry Irish heart and is as charged with ambition as a twenty-year-old. The praise of critics and a bustling box office have had a predictable effect: Meara is hard at work on another play.

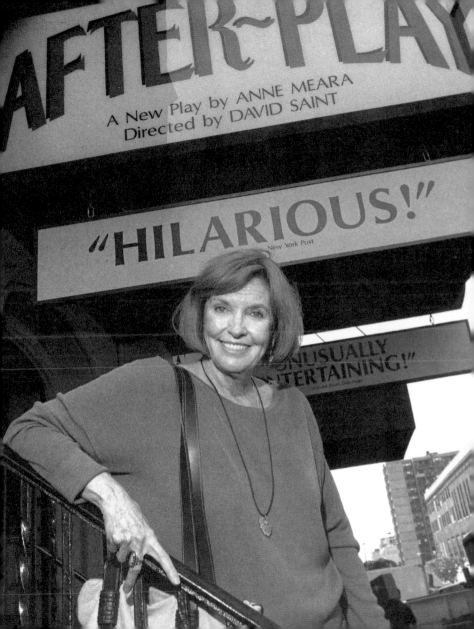

WELL, AND SO THERE WE ARE! Astonishing, is it not, to observe how many different pathways lead to the same goal of self-fulfillment? And numerous as those pathways appear to be, we do well to remember that they are only a tiny fraction of the whole. It is in the nature of history to single out certain persons and grant them fame, but the majority of people who have successfully realized their ambitions go unremarked, and perhaps for that very reason: having achieved within the conventional boundaries of a given time and place what they sought to achieve, they have seen no reason to court fame; instead they have slipped into a well-earned obscurity, one that for all we know to the contrary was very welcome to them.

As time passes, this mighty army of the obscure is reduced to names and dates carved in stone in some rarely visited churchyard. What they were like as individuals may persist in the memory of their families for two or three generations—save in exceptional cases, not more. Surely our ancestors laughed, but the sound of their laughter is probably the first of their characteristics to be lost to us; they must have wept, but their tears, too, are lost. To an extent that we are unable to measure, we are shaped by their personalities as well as by their genes, and it is for our sakes, in order to identify ourselves, that we seek to lure them back out of anonymity.

Despite our best efforts, most of us fail to find any useful clues to self-knowledge in the scanty family information handed down to us. Of a long-dead great-grandfather we learn only that his favorite song was *The Camptown Races*, or of an equally long-dead great-grandmother only that she had blue eyes and a sharp tongue. Necessarily, we turn to the lives of people, strangers to us, who have managed to enter history and assume a commanding posture there. Many of them stand clustered together in this book by dint of a single attribute—that of having taken a long time to be embraced by fame. We pay them the compliment of calling them late bloomers, and now, as a further compliment, we may wish to choose from among them two or three ideal pretend ancestors, taking the place of those real ancestors about whom, to our sorrow, we know so little.

Which of the distinguished men and women described in these pages would you care to select a place for high up in the branches of your family tree? Kindly, irresistible Montaigne? Brusque Swift? That witty rascal Sterne? (Once safely dead, rascals are much sought-after as ancestors.) Take your pick, and have no undue fear of being rejected by them. For it is possible that they, too, have a family search under way—that they are as eagerly in pursuit of descendants as we are of ancestors. If so, they need not waste another precious moment of their eternities. Smiling, we hold out our hands to them.

Photo Credits

Front Cover, Clockwise from Top Left: Julia Child, UPI / Bettmann;
Harry Truman, UPI / Bettmann; Coco Chanel, UPI / Bettmann;
Harland Sanders, © Karsh / Woodfin Camp & Associates, Inc.

Back Cover: Susan Woldenberg

Berenice Abbott / Commerce Graphics Ltd, Inc. • **113**

Courtesy American Theatre Wing • **133**

Archive Photos • **15, 35, 75, 111, 117**

Jerry Bauer • **87**

The Bettmann Archive • **37, 57, 85, 99, 125, 137, 153**

Courtesy Beyer Blinder Belle • **145**

Richard Falco / Black Star • **69**

Brown Brothers • **65**

Marc Bryan-Brown • **101**

Bryn Mawr College Archives • **81**

Culver Pictures • **29, 71, 95, 103, 109, 121, 127, 159**

Courtesy André Emmerich Gallery • **97**

Bill Evans • **143**

Jill Gill • **141**

Globe Photos, Inc. • **33, 73, 83, 149**

Merwin Goldsmith • **161**

The Granger Collection • **47, 51, 61, 79, 93, 107, 147, 157**

James Hamilton • **67**

Courtesy Al Hirschfeld • **139**

The Hulton Deutsch Collection • **31, 123**

© Karsh / Woodfin Camp & Associates, Inc. • **21, 41 45, 89, 115**

Paul Lerner / Woodfin Camp & Associates, Inc. • **25**

Photography by Alec Marshall. Courtesy Architectural Digest © 1992 The Condé Nast

Publications. All rights reserved. Used with permission. • **105**

Courtesy Moorland-Spingarn Research Center, Howard University.

Photographer: Fabian Bachrach • **129**

Charles H. Bayley Picture and Painting Fund, and partial Gift of Elizabeth Paine Metcalf

Courtesy of Museum of Fine Arts, Boston • **19** (Detail)

© 1986 Arnold Newman • **131, 155**

Pepperidge Farm, Inc. • **91**

© 1996 Sylvia Plachy • **23, 77**

Peter Pollack 1966, Whitney Museum of American Art, Library • **49**

Veryl Oakland / Retna Ltd • **55**

Scavullo • **39**

Department of Special Collections, University Research Library, UCLA • **151**

UPI / Bettmann • **17, 27, 53, 59, 63, 135**

Index

BOOK CONCEPT AND DESIGN BY DENNIS AND SUSAN FEIGENBAUM
THE TEXT WAS SET IN TRUMP MEDIEVAL AND FUTURA
THE DISPLAY TYPE IS ISADORA SCRIPT
PRINTED AND BOUND BY MANDARIN OFFSET, HONG KONG